Mike & Jill Gagliano

Dr. Frank W. Cho

Oh My Love, Cambodia

JOURNAL OF AN EARLY-RETIRED DENTIST'S
SECOND LIFE AS A MISSIONARY

| Frank W. Cho |

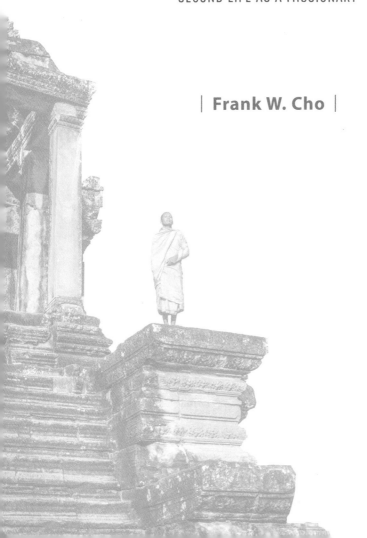

LITTLE MUSTARD SEED

Oh My Love, Cambodia

Copyright © 2021 by Frank W. Cho

Published by Little Mustard Seed, Inc.

Little Mustard Seed, Inc.
1540 Lorella Avenue
La Habra, California 90631
Phone: 714-401-8697 / 714-213-6980
Email: drfcho@gmail.com

ISBN: 978-0-9863510-6-8

Printed in Korea

In loving memory of my mentor,

Kenneth K. Kim, DDS

Angkor Wat is a temple complex that was constructed over a period of 30 years by Khmer Emperor, Suryavarman II. Angkor Wat consists of large mountainous towers that are surrounded by cloisters. The towers represent Mount Meru, home of the Buddhist gods.

ANGKOR WAT

CONTENTS

1

Recommendations

Dr. Frank and Tina Cho's missionary story and love for Cambodia is extraordinary and inspiring as they served the people of Cambodia after the "killing fields" genocide in the late 1970's.

Dr. Frank and Tina Cho's dedication to Christian missions and the furthering of God's Kingdom through dentistry, Christian education, and church planting has positively impacted multitudes of dental professionals, students, and patients for many years. Dr. Frank has been a member of the Christian Dental Society (CDS) since 1978 while in dental school and has served on the CDS Advisory Council since 1997. In 1993, in response to a plea from the CDS for volunteers to teach at the only Cambodian dental school, Dr. Frank and Tina had a call and a vision to become full-time, Christian dental missionaries to Cambodia. In preparation, Dr. Frank attended Fuller Seminary before departing for Cambodia in 2004 with the support of Church Resources Ministry and $15,000 from CDS. In May 2005, he opened a dental clinic in Phnom Penh to help the poor, to evangelize, and to teach dental students. He established a dental lab in 2007 and has taught at the International University Dental School since 2008. Mrs. Tina Cho worked as office manager and taught Cambodian assistants while Dr. Frank trained dental students.

Dr. Frank and Tina led approximately six, portable, short-term, dental Christian outreach mission trips each year for 11 years, treating about 900-1,500 patients on each trip. Many CDS members, to include myself and my wife, participated on Dr. Cho's trips and saw first-hand how dentistry effectively provided physical healing to open the doors to Christian hope for the oppressed. The teams utilized full-time evangelists and taught team members how to share the Gospel with small groups waiting for dental treatment. Dr. Frank gave evangelistic messages to the patients he treated.

Dr. Frank and Tina hosted Bible studies in their dental office and in their home as they mentored dental students and others, some of whom came to the Lord, were baptized, and now attend and serve in churches. Dr. Frank served as Church Elder and Tina taught children as they ministered with a local Cambodian pastor to the poor. They helped under-resourced people who lived in tarp tents in the hot sun following home evictions and their church built 150 hut houses for these families.

Dr. Frank and Tina used their skills of dentistry, teaching, evangelism, and dental clinicity to bring the hope of Jesus to many Cambodians in a predominantly Buddhist society. They dedicated themselves, heart and soul, to fulfilling the Great Commission, and have done so with humility and love.

Dr. Frank and Tina Cho represent incredible examples of self-sacrifices, arduous labors, and heroic efforts in using their God-given gifts to reach the spiritual and physical needs of the poor as full-time missionaries after early retirement from a private dental practice. Their contributions to Christianity, to dentistry, to missions, to their church community, and to Cambodia are unparalleled and make for inspirational reading in their book, "Oh my love, Cambodia."

Respectfully Submitted by,

Dr. Robert D. Meyer
Executive Director of the Christian Dental Society
Colonel (Retired) Robert D. Meyer, DMD, MAGD, ABGD, FADI

2

In early March 2004 I received an email from Dr. Frank Cho. At that time I was the team leader for a small group of missionaries serving with InnerCHANGE in Cambodia. In his email of just 272 words Dr. Frank explained that both he and his wife, Tina, had recently retired and felt called to serve in the mission field in Cambodia. Rarely have I received such a short email that would have such a large and long-lasting impact on our team, on the neighborhoods where InnerCHANGE works, and on the poor and marginalized throughout Cambodia.

Dr. Frank's email kicked off our correspondence which led to the Chos joining InnerCHANGE, living among and serving the poor and marginalized in Cambodia. I was amazed by the story that unfolded, including dreams and visions given to the Chos, the Chos responding in faith with little certainty of where God was leading them, and God's love and compassion being poured through them onto many throughout this land.

And this impact continues today as the many, many people Tina and Dr. Frank touched during their time in Cambodia now extend their healing touch to others, whether in the local church, as dental workers, or as loving neighbors.

When I think about Dr. Frank and Tina four words come immediately to mind: listen, learn, laugh and love. Even though the Chos had a successful dental practice in the US along with all the comforts that one could hope for, Dr. Frank and Tina were listening for God's words—their marching orders—which they heard, tested, and obeyed. Their obedience is a moving example to inspire us all towards waiting upon the Lord and acting upon His word.

The Chos exemplified a learning posture throughout their time in Cambodia, diligently laboring to learn Cambodian language and culture to closely connect with their neighbors and dental colleagues, and more importantly to communicate His truths in powerful and appropriate ways. Perhaps even more stretching, at times, was fitting into a multicultural team of younger InnerCHANGE missionaries. Though the challenges of learning Cambodian culture and team culture were demanding, in a country that is very hot and lacking most amenities, Dr. Frank and Tina were always able to extend grace and demonstrate humor as they worked through difficulties. They gifted our team with great joy, laughter, and wisdom that comes with experience.

Finally, love. One cannot help but be inspired by 1 Corinthians 13. This entire chapter should be on the role description for every missionary, but especially verses 1 Corinthians 13:4-7:

"Love is patient, love is kind. It does not envy, it does not boast, it is not proud. It does not dishonor others, it is not self-seeking, it is not easily angered, it keeps no record of wrongs. Love does not delight in evil but rejoices with the truth. It always protects, always trusts, always hopes, always perseveres."

Dr. Frank and Tina embody this for me, and I am a better servant because of being blessed with the opportunity to serve shoulder to shoulder with them, to listen with them, to learn and laugh with them, and to be impelled to greater acts of love for others through their example.

I hope this book inspires you to listen for your marching orders, to learn and laugh along the way, and to join with Dr. Frank's and Tina's example to love deeply those whom God puts in your path.

Grace and peace,

Mark Smith
Country Director, InnerCHANGE Cambodia

3

It was my pleasure to work with Dr. Frank Cho during his 14 years in Cambodia. I was former Dean at the Faculty of Dentistry, International University for much of that time, and Frank became an important part of our Faculty, beginning in 2007. Frank taught mainly fixed and removable prosthodontics, but also some periodontics and endodontics. At that time we had very few dental specialists in Cambodia, and so Frank's knowledge and skills were greatly needed.

Frank was known as a strict teacher. Students who arrived late for class would miss the test he often gave as soon as the bell rang – and if he observed anyone cheating they would be immediately evicted from the class. At first this was a shock for students, but they soon realized that Frank wanted them to be the best they could be, and needed to learn discipline. He demanded high standards both in the classroom and in the clinic. It is a tribute to Frank that many of his top former students, following graduation, went on to do postgraduate study—some in Cambodia and some in Thailand. Those students are now among the leaders of dentistry in this country.

Outside the classroom, Frank offered the students additional help in the form of seminars and study clubs. Frank showed that he really cared for the students. He was not just interested in their academic success. He developed strong relationships with many students, got to know their individual situations, and supported their physical, mental and spiritual needs. Frank was also involved with prison outreach, involving dental students from two of the dental schools. Over the years he gained the love and respect of many generations of dental students.

During his final 3 years in Cambodia Frank entered the Master of Endodontics program with three of his former students. He worked hard and became part of a close-knit group who supported each other during their studies. Whenever I meet with these young dentists, they speak very highly of Frank. All three of them are Christian, thanks in large part to Frank's evangelism. On the day of their thesis defense at International University, it was uplifting to see Frank and the 3 Cambodian graduates joining together in a prayer of thanks in front of their teachers, friends, colleagues and students.

During his time in Cambodia I always saw Frank as a "man with a mission." A mission to help improve the quality of dental education in Cambodia, a mission to bring basic dental services to the poor, and a mission to share the good news.

Frank has made an important contribution to the people of Cambodia, especially young people. I thank God for Frank and Tina, and would like them to know that their legacy lives on within the people they have touched during their 14 years of service in Cambodia.

Dr. Callum Durward
Dean of University of Puthisastra
Faculty of Dentistry

4

Love and passion are the words that come to mind immediately when I think about Dr. Frank and Tina Cho. For 14 years I have witnessed their passion for the gospel and their love for Cambodian people. They loved the Cambodians so much that they gave up their comfortable lives, moved to Cambodia to open dental clinics, and went to remote places to provide dental care and education to raise up future dentists in Cambodia.

It was about 2004 when I met them for the first time. The condition of dental facilities in Cambodia at that time was very poor, making it difficult for patients to receive proper care. Many patients were hopeless as they could not afford the cost of dental treatments. This was quite a different environment then what Dr. Frank and Tina were accustomed to. I'm sure the food and climates in Cambodia were very foreign to them. Regardless, they lived in Cambodia loving and serving the people.

In 2005, Dr. Frank and Tina opened a dental clinic at the military dental clinic in Phnom Penh. I was very touched to see how they were serving and helping the patients who were living in poverty. I have the utmost respect for them and how they faithfully lived out a holistic missionary life for 14 years with their profession in one hand and the gospel in the other.

There are three things that I want to share about them.

First, they are people of sacrificial love that remind me of both the sacrifice Christ has made on the cross and the verse from John 3:16 "God so loved the world". Dr. Frank had a team that specifically went to remote and underdeveloped areas of Cambodia and one of our church-plants had the privilege of partnering with him and his team. I vividly remember one particular day when the team had set up a temporary treatment center on top of a dirt road, working relentlessly under extremely hot weather all day, from early morning till late afternoon, caring for the patients. That to me was an example of sacrificial love.

Second, they were investors in the future generation. They did not limit their ministry to treating patients, but invested great effort in raising the next generation of dentists in Cambodia. They supported the dental students with scholarships and passionately taught and trained the students and trainees at the dental school.

Third, they set a great example as tent-makers. As professional dentists, not only did they use their talents to treat patients, teach and train the students, they also shared the message of the gospel as they lived out the life of Christ's love and sacrifice.

Lastly, if I were to summarize their lives as missionaries in Cambodia into one sentence, I can confidently say that they lived a life that exalted Jesus (Philippians 1:20). I give thanks to Dr. Frank and Tina Cho once again for their sacrificial love and passion shown for the land of Cambodia.

Peter Kong
Current OMF Director of South Korea,
Former OMF Missionary of Cambodia.

5

We met Dr. Frank in Cambodia in 2004. Over the years he and his wife, Tina, have become very dear friends to us. They care deeply for the people of Cambodia especially towards the poor and needy. When children with HIV were rejected by the other clinics for treatment, Dr. Frank welcomed them with open arms and gave them quality dental treatment without discrimination. He set up dental clinics in partnership with mission organisations to provide free dental treatment or at a minimal fee for those who are poor. Dr. Frank also helped to look for scholarships and personally gave some of his own money to support the tuition fees of a few needy dental students and trained them up personally so that they could be equipped as competent dentists.

Both he and Tina have a kingdom perspective: they seek to witness to non-Christian staff and students, have regular Bible studies with staff, organise dental missions to the poor and needy communities in the provinces, encouraged and shared his dental knowledge with the Cambodian Christian dentists that meet as a fellowship, and they also served in the International church in Phnom Penh.

Age is just a number for Dr. Frank. He studied for his Master's in Endodontics in a Cambodian university when he was 70 years old. This challenges us who are younger not to just sit back but to continue to be stretched in our minds and in our service. Dr. Frank never let age be the defining factor, even after "retiring" as a dentist in USA, he continued to serve for 14 years in Cambodia. Indeed Dr. Frank is like what the psalmist mentioned in Psalm 103:5, "He fulfills the desires of your heart so that your strength is renewed like the eagle's". Dr. Frank has left an indelible legacy in our hearts and in the hearts of many Cambodians.

Dr. Yewon & Chern Chern Choo
OMF Missionaries in Cambodia

6

As founding member of Global Dental Alliance (GDA), previously known as Korean American Christian Dental Missions (KACDM), Dr. Cho has been a leader, fellow worker, and a supporter of our organization for the last three decades. Other dental professionals in our group, myself included, have admired the way that Dr. Cho utilizes his dental profession as a tool to spread the gospel in remote places in the world.

Dr. Frank Cho and his wife, Tina, serve as a great example of what sacrifice and serving our Lord overseas looks like. They took an early retirement from their private practice in California to become full-time dental missionaries in Cambodia.

GDA has worked closely with Dr. Cho and many of our members have gone on short-term mission trips to Cambodia in corroboration with Dr. Cho. After the trips, our members always returned with positive reports and inspiring stories.

On behalf of GDA, I am excited for people to enjoy this beautiful compilation of Frank Cho's missionary journey, and I trust that many will be inspired by his stories.

Blessings,

John H. Kim, DDS
GDA President

7

We have known Frank and Tina Cho since their arrival in Cambodia in 2004. As dentists and felllow missionaries in Cambodia, we had the opportunity to partner in ministry together. Frank and Tina demonstrated a wonderful servant attitude as they served Cambodians. They provided quality dental treatment to countless poor and many missionaries. Frank also trained and mentored many dental students. Frank welcomed me to serve alongside him at Mercy Dental clinic in the capital city and during some of his many mission trips to the provinces.

While serving, they unashamedly and lovingly shared the gospel message. The Chos have left a legacy of love that many Cambodians will remember.

Kreg Mallow, DDS
Kreg and Jenny Mallow have served as missionaries
in Cambodia for 30 years with World Concern and OMF

Author Prologue

The stories that are shared in this book are from my mission journal to Cambodia from 2004 to 2018. I spent the prime years of my life in the United States where I established and operated my own dental clinic. I definitely enjoyed the countless benefits of living in the most developed country in the world, America, also known as the land of opportunity. Then, at the age of 50, I felt the call to become a missionary. After putting much thought and prayer into this call, my wife and I decided to retire early. It took about 10 years to prepare ourselves for our early retirement and full-time missions in Cambodia. Finally, at the age of 60, the time to leave for Cambodia had come.

This book is a record of our 14 years of burning passion and deep love for the land of Cambodia. The reason I was able to spend a huge part of my 60s and 70s in a very foreign place was the grace of Jesus and the gospel provided to me through the cross. As the Apostle Paul confessed, "I am obligated both to Greeks and non-Greeks..." (Romans 1:14, NIV), we were more than happy to share our talents and the gospel of life with the people of Cambodia without limit. The 14 years of life spent in Cambodia were a huge privilege for us.

This record of our personal stories may be somewhat insignificant, but it is a record of our observations and experiences as professional dental missionaries. There are three reasons for making this memoir. First, this memoir is to help in any way those who are considering and praying about full-time missions after early retirement as professionals. Second, it is to inspire and motivate young medical / dental professionals to start dreaming for missions. And third, it is to help those who are wondering how to partake in God's kingdom as a tent-maker and through "Business as Missions." I hope and pray that this book will encourage and challenge those of you who are interested in dental missions.

I would like to thank Elder Kenneth K. Kim, DDS (The Korean Open Door Church). "Record before you forget" is what Kenneth said that motivated and pushed me to write this book. I also thank all the members of our home church, mission organizations, and churches that have supported us both in prayer and finances for 14 years. As long as my memory lives, I will remember them and be forever grateful.

I also give thanks to my beloved wife, who has faithfully supported me as a wife and a co-worker for God's kingdom. My four loving daughters, Connie, Mimi, Rosemary, Christine, who have also deeply supported me for many years.

Lastly, I give thanks to Pastor Andy Sunwoong Kim, the President of Mustard Seed Bible Institution, for helping me from beginning to end to publish this book. I give all the glory, gratitude, and honor to our Triune God.

April 30, 2020
Dr. Frank and Tina Cho

PART 1

Dream Towards the New Continent

"

Praise be to the God and Father of our Lord Jesus Christ, who has blessed us in the heavenly realms with every spiritual blessing in Christ. For he chose us in him before the creation of the world to be holy and blameless in his sight. In love he predestined us for adoption to sonship through Jesus Christ, in accordance with his pleasure and will—to the praise of his glorious grace, which he has freely given us in the One he loves. In him we have redemption through his blood, the forgiveness of sins, in accordance with the riches of God's grace (Ephesians 1:3-7, NIV).

1

Immeasurable Experience

Repentance of an Elderly Woman

Let me start my book with a story of a grandmother who became a widow at a young age. One day, Pastor Sungsoo Hwang's father assistant Pastor Boik Hwang (who was a politician in Korea) escorted Presbyterian Church in the United States (PCUS) missionary Boyer to tour the Gohung region (the PCUS Mission Headquarters was located Soonchun city).

At that time, this grandmother was working in a rice paddy field plucking weeds. As Boyer and assistant Pastor Hwang unexpectedly approached the elderly woman, she stopped what she was doing and listened to the gospel Boyer was sharing. As soon as the gospel was presented to her, she knelt down and accepted Jesus as her Lord and Savior. That elderly woman's name was Goeup Park and her repentance and belief in Jesus became the seed of the gospel in my family. God had used one person's repentance to begin His gospel work in an entire family.

What an amazing blessing that was! The Apostle Paul said in Galatians 1:15-16, "But when God, who set me apart from my mother's womb and called me by his grace, was pleased to reveal his Son in me so that I might preach him among the Gentiles, my immediate response was not to consult any human being" (NIV). Just as the Apostle Paul testified and rejoiced in God's grace, His salvation and calling started in my family from the repentance of my grandmother. In a similar way as the Apostle Paul, I cannot help but praise God for His love and perfect plan!

After my grandmother Goeup accepted Jesus into her life, she began to worship God and serve Him through Dohwa Church. According to my father, my grandmother tried to wholeheartedly live out her love for and faith in Jesus. It was one of her deep desires and prayers that her future daughter-in-law would be a believer in Jesus Christ. So, my grandmother prayed and prayed and prayed, and God was faithful to answer her prayers! God sent my mother (Bong-soon Shin), a firm believer in Jesus, as a gift to our family. In the same way, we can always experience this good God who faithfully answers our prayers when we pray according His will.

Birth and Growth

As mentioned before, my mother was a devout follower of Jesus. My father, In-hong Cho, was not a follower of Jesus at the time of his marriage to my mother. My father and mother had a total of six children—three boys and three girls. I am the fifth child out of the six children! I was born on December 9, 1941 in Ok-ha Ri, Go-hung, Jeonnam, Korea. I grew up going to Go-hung Eup Church. The senior pastor of that church was Pastor Kyu-oh Jung. Later he became the senior pastor at Kwangju Central Church and faithfully served churches of the Honam area. The missionary Boyer regularly made visits to Go-hung churches and helped us grow as disciples of Jesus Christ. I remember one day when Doctor Jarvis, a missionary from the United States, came to lead a revival meeting at a high school campus in Soonchun. I can still vividly remember seeing my grandmother singing the hymn "At the Hill of Gethsemane" in front of over 600 people at that revival meeting. My grandmother must have been a very extroverted and talented person!

Then one day, upon our senior Pastor Jung, Kyu-oh's recommendation, my sister and I moved with his two children to another city called Soon-chun for middle and high school. Although my sister and I were apart from our family, whenever we came back to our hometown of Go-hung, we never failed to follow our mother to early dawn service every morning. I still cannot forget my mother's love for Jesus and faithful, consistent prayers. When my father's business was not doing well, our family moved to Pajoo near the Demilitarized Zone, where my oldest brother was working. As a result, I had to finish high school on my own. Thankfully, I was accepted to dental school at Kyung Hee University in Seoul and completed my collegiate studies there.

Dreams to Success

As soon as I graduated from dental school, I moved to California in 1975. My sister had already immigrated to California in 1965 and paved the way for me to transition there as well. I truly believe that this was also a part of God's perfect plan. If I had lived in Korea, I believe my dreams would have been very small and limited. When I came to the United States, I devoted myself to studying and mastering the English language. All that hard work paid off and I was able to transfer to the International Student Program (ISP) at the University of Southern California (USC) Dental School. By the grace of God, I got accepted as one of 20 people who had an international dentist license already. I completed the ISP program in 1978 and started working at a dental office for the next six months. Then, I opened a dental clinic in Bell Gardens, California in January of 1979.

It is solely by God's grace that He led such an insignificant person like me to come to America, complete my studies at USC, and open a dental clinic.

Picture of the family of missionary Frank Cho, his wife, and the families of his four daughters —Connie, Mimi, Rosemary, and Christine

Opening a Dental Clinic in the United States

I married my wife, Tina Cho, in 1972 and had four daughters, Connie, Mimi, Rosemary, and Christine. I started attending Westminster Presbyterian Church, currently called Orange Hill Presbyterian Church, in 1976. For the next 23 years, from April 1979 to August 2002, I worked as a dentist, caring for my patients, as well as serving as an elder at my church. Now that I look back in hindsight, I can see how God was slowly but surely moving me along through His plan to call me as a full-time missionary.

EXPERIENCING CAMBODIAN CULTURE

Tradition of Matriarchal Society

Cambodian culture has long been a matriarchal society. When a man marries a woman, he joins his wife's side of the family to live and work as a farmer on their land. This is opposite of the Confucian society that puts emphasis on the male. More than 90% of the population in Cambodia are farmers, so the matriarchal society is still ongoing today. In this society, the wives are the absolute authority in the family. Wives are the owners of the family businesses and the husbands are their supporters. The family assets, however, are shared by both. The matriarchal society is now comparably weaker than before, but the tradition of a man living in the home of their in-laws for two to three months still exists. This is very natural for the Cambodians. The power of wives in the family is strong, whereas the politics and military is men's territory.

Bride and groom washing the feet of parents at a Christian wedding in Cambodia

"

Even though I was once a blasphemer and a persecutor and a violent man, I was shown mercy because I acted in ignorance and unbelief. The grace of our Lord was poured out on me abundantly, along with the faith and love that are in Christ Jesus. Here is a trustworthy saying that deserves full acceptance: Christ Jesus came into the world to save sinners—of whom I am the worst (1 Timothy 1:13-15, NIV).

2

Calling and Preparation

Member Registration at CDS

In 1979, I was working at my dental clinic in Bell Gardens, giving my undivided attention and care to my patients. As I was studying at USC, I met my mentor by the name of Kennth K. Kim. We participated in the California Dental Association Convention in Anaheim together. We were looking around at the various booths, when we visited the Christian Dental Society (CDS) booth. Kennth stopped, turned around and said to me, "Hey, I am a member of CDS. Do you want to be a member of this mission organization? CDS is a very good mission organization!" It was that one question that sparked the beginning of my journey with CDS. What a pivotal moment because who knew then that I would be going out as a full-time missionary to Cambodia decades later? Only God, in His sovereignty and foreknowledge, knew that I would join CDS and be sent off to Cambodia. God knows our beginning and our end; His mission (Missio Dei) is so fearfully and wonderfully planned and carried out.

Calling as a Missionary to Cambodia

Ever since I opened my dental clinic in 1976, I had a subscription to the L.A. Times. So, I would read all the news, but it was always the articles concerning Cambodia that grabbed my attention. My heart for Cambodia grew as I learned about the genocide in 1975 and its unstable politics and economy. In 1975, communists invaded Phnom Phen and massacred the majority of the nation's intellectuals and the Vietnamese people. With the ongoing genocide by the communists in Cambodia, the L.A. Times continued to monitor and to report on this terrible news. This led me to be more intentionally aware of Cambodia and I began to pray for her people.

Through the Paris Negotiation in 1993, over 20 years of civil war in Cambodia finally came to an end. Cambodia, then, went under the reign and oversight of the United Nations (U.N.) for the next one and a half years. During the 20 years of the civil war, medical and dental schools were unfortunately closed. Therefore, the United Nations charged World Concern, a Christian global relief and development organization, with the task of re-opening medical and dental schools in Cambodia. In turn, World Concern asked CDS, a dental mission organization, to help with the task of opening and establishing dental schools in Cambodia. CDS agreed to help in this endeavor.

Ever since 1993, my heart for Cambodia had been growing steadily. Around this time, I received a newsletter from CDS saying they were looking for early retirees to join on as dental missionaries. I was already familiar with CDS because I was serving in this organization since college. With this newsletter, something stirred in my heart—an affirmation of God's calling to go to Cambodia. I immediately shared this desire with my wife. She affirmed the call of God to go to Cambodia and agreed to support this vision that God had placed in my heart.

Some time later, I met Ron Lamb at a CDS annual meeting. When I met Ron Lamb, my vision for missions to Cambodia materialized and solidified more concretely. As a former president of CDS, Ron had been going to Cambodia from 1992 to 1995, a total of three trips, in order to help build and start a dental school. After meeting Ron, I began to pray fervently and consistently about long-term missions.

However, it took 10 years for me to be confident and sure that it was God's sovereign timing to retire and leave for Cambodia. In these 10 years I earnestly sought and asked for God's wisdom. I prayed, "Lord, what do I need to do right now in order to prepare for missions to Cambodia 10 years later? Teach me! Guide me!" And God faithfully answered my prayers.

Cambodia was a place I had always had an interest in and prayed for. My general prayer for this nation, however, had gradually become more specific. I prayed for a vision of becoming a dental missionary to Cambodia and God poured out His grace to make that vision become reality in my life. Furthermore, the joy of this vision doubled when my wife began to walk alongside me—walking towards the same goal, same path, same vision for Cambodia.

As I began to pray for missions to Cambodia, I asked Pastor Hyang-gun Lee, my friend from Soonchun Maesan Middle School and missionary of Partner International in Los Angeles, to introduce me to a missionary in Cambodia whom I could support financially and with prayer. My friend Hyanggun introduced me to a pastor named Timothy Ith. As a small group leader in my church, I led our group to pray for him and the country of Cambodia whenever I led our meetings. Through these opportunities, God was preparing us to go to Cambodia. Pastor Ith was a refugee from Cambodia, who flew to Modesto, California. He started working as an

Pastor Timothy Ith baptizing Dr. Makar

aviation mechanic there and attended a Baptist seminary. After he was ordained, Pastor Ith went back to Cambodia and served his country as a spiritual leader. I encouraged my church, Orange Hill Presbyterian Church, to partner and support Pastor Ith. As a result, my church supported Pastor Ith both financially and with prayer for the next nine years, until my wife and I went to Cambodia as full-time missionaries. Together a local pastor by the name of Hang Abraham Simting and I pioneered and started a local church in Cambodia. It was, then, that Pastor Ith, who served as president of Evangelical Fellowship of Cambodia (EFC), came to participate in baptizing members of this local church. Pastor Ith was our intimate helper during the 14-years that my wife and I were in Cambodia.

Preparation for Missions to Cambodia

I knew that going to Cambodia in the second half of my life would prove to be a great challenge. From 1993 on, I began to devote myself fully to preparing for full-time missions for the next 10 years. This preparation involved two aspects: Firstly, a plan of what we would do on the mission field, and secondly, a financial plan and path for early retirement and theological training in seminary.

Theological training was the most important part of the preparation since I had to be ready to teach the Word of God. It was equally important, however, to plan ahead and be prepared financially after retiring from our mission to Cambodia. I also needed to build a strong relationship with the missions organization that I hoped would commission us—CDS.

The very first step that I took was financial preparation. The best and the most traditional way of preparing for finances and retirement was through savings. Therefore, I started a Define Benefit Pension Fund, which was the most beneficial 401(k) plan for doctors, and began saving and contributing to this fund. In this plan the employer pays for all employees. The employees do not pay at all. With those funds, I was able to purchase the building that my dental clinic was located in as a part of our retirement nest egg. Tina and I really committed ourselves to save as much money as possible. Fortunately, at the time of opening, there was a shortage of dentists and dental clinics around the area. Therefore, we received many clients, which allowed us to save money faster than expected.

Next, I tried my best to build a stronger bond with CDS. As a collegiate student, I had registered as a member of CDS and maintained my membership by paying dues. However, that was the extent of my involvement—I was never really active and rarely participated in their meetings. I had to change this because I wanted to be commissioned by CDS. Therefore, I did my best to commu-nicate this God-given calling and passion for Cambodian mis-sions to the members of CDS. At that time, I was serving at another dental mission organi-zation called KACDM (later changed to

Korean American Christian Dental Mission visiting Prey Veng

Global Dental Alliance in 2016) as a treasurer. I went on several GDA dental missions to Mexico at this time, so it was very stretching for me to serve in both CDS and GDA. Yet, I persistently and faithfully served, and continued to build relationships with CDS. Finally, in 2004, I was ordained, commissioned, and sent off by CDS. Throughout the prepa-ration period, I participated in all the general meetings and events, as well as short-term missions to Honduras, which was very memorable.

"

Trust in the Lord with all your heart and lean not on your own understanding; in all your ways submit to him, and he will make your paths straight. Do not be wise in your own eyes; fear the Lord and shun evil. This will bring health to your body and nourishment to your bones. Honor the Lord with your wealth, with the firstfruits of all your crops; then your barns will be filled to overflowing, and your vats will brim over with new wine (Proverbs 3:5-10, NIV).

3

Spiritual Arming

Fuller Seminary

After I received the call to be a missionary in 1993, I started training in three areas. In the previous chapter, I talked about the financial preparations to plan for early retirement, as well as developing the relationship with CDS as a sending organization.

In this chapter, I want to talk about the third aspect of preparation: the theological preparation which was two years, from September 2002 to July 2004.

I had known and always admired professor Seyoon Kim of Fuller Seminary. Professor Seyoon had come to our church to do a seminar on salvation and the essence of the gospel. I remember being shocked by the clarity of his teaching. It was then that I decided that I had to take his Pauline Theology class at Fuller Seminary. I retired in August 2002, and in the very next month, I visited Fuller Seminary in order to enroll in professor Seyoon's Pauline Theology class. Unfortunately, I was not able to take his class because I had not taken any of the prerequisites

Professor Dr. Seyoon Kim from Fuller Seminary in Pasadena (Left) and Reverend Andy Sunwoong Kim (President of Mustard Seed Bible Institution)

that were required. Initially, I wanted to take individual classes, but I decided to fully enroll and take all the classes.

For my first semester, I took the following classes: New Testament Theology, Hermeneutics, and Spiritual Formation. The New Testament Theology class was great because it reminded me of how Christ's death and resurrection was the good news of God to the entire world. The Hermeneutics class was an opportunity for me to study and meditate upon the whole Bible. Through this course, the Bible not only became a tool for me to teach others, but also a living and active weapon for me to arm myself with the Word of God. In this class, we focused on the book of 2 Corinthians.

Lastly, through the Spiritual Formation class, I learned from the lives of spiritual giants throughout church history. This course taught me how to be more like Christ, especially through prayer and meditation on the Word. It was a time that helped me to wrestle with the spiritual formation of my soul into praxis, the application of theological truths into my day-to-day life.

I received another confirmation to go as a full-time missionary to Cambodia during my time at Fuller Seminary—I met professor Jude Tiersma Watson (then a member of the Church Resources Ministry, now Novo). This meeting was a pivotal moment. God is always faithful; He is without error. I am confident that it was God who led me to professor Watson and her class in Spiritual Formation. My time in her Spiritual Formation class was where I truly experienced God who provides and prepares.

On the last day of the Spiritual Formation class, professor Jude Watson asked something to the students. She asked, "What are you going to do after you graduate?" The whole class was asked to write down the plan and without any hesitation, I wrote that I would go to Cambodia as a full-time missionary. Then, professor Watson called me to her office a week later and suggested looking into serving through CRM which she was a part of. She said the InnerCHANGE Department was already doing ministry in Cambodia since 1993, and suggested I look into CRM if I had not decided on the commissioning mission organization. I did not ultimately take Professor Watson's offer to join CRM because their focus on ministry to the poor was not quite in sync with my focus on teaching

Professor Jude Tiersma Watson

at a dental school and doing dental missions. But, in Chapter 4, I will dive more in depth into how my meeting with professor Jude Watson affected and shaped my life and my missions.

Through these unexpected experiences and meetings, God prepared me, armed me spiritually, and trained me to trust God and follow His direction. God already knew every minute detail of my journey to Cambodia and led me step-by-step without any mistake or error.

Brief History of Cambodia

Before we go on with the vision trip to Cambodia, let me now share a brief history of Cambodia.

Khmer was not different from any of the other neighboring kingdoms. In AD 802, Jayavarman II, the king of Siem Reap, established the Angkor Empire and started to conquer its neighboring countries in the region, thus marking a place in history as a powerful empire. The authority and fame of the Angkor Empire reached its peak in the 12th century (1113-1150) under the reign of Suryavarman II. The territory had reached the border of present-day Thailand, Laos, and the Tang dynasty of China. Even the Delta region that covers Ho Chi Minh City and the Mekong River were under the reign of Suryavarman II.

In AD 1165, a special force of the Cham Empire from mid-Vietnam and an anti-government group attacked the capital city of Angkor Empire. Upon their victory from this unexpected campaign, this group reigned the Empire for four years. As Vietnam grew in power, the Cham Empire was abolished and the Delta region was overtaken. This resulted in Vietnam taking control over Cambodians in that region. Even to this day, the majority of the population in the western part of the Vietnamese border is ethnically Cambodian.

After this, Thailand and Laos consecutively became independent from the Angkor Empire. The independence of the countries that were under Angkor control was the final reason for the weakening of its power. After a while, the whole Cham tribe converted to Islam and with the permission of Angkor Empire moved to Cambodia. Today they live as fisherman around the region of Mekong River. The population of the Cham tribe is around 400,000. They have their own language as well.

Thailand overtook the western Battambang, which is a present-day granary. "Under the oppression of Thailand, Cambodia frequently moved its capital. France established a protectorate over Cambodia and with France's strong pressure, Thailand returned a portion of Battam-

*Angkor Wat as seen from the doorway in
Siem Reap, Cambodia*

bang. With construction of the new royal palace in 1866, Cambodia moved its capital to Phnom Penh.

King Norodom Sihanouk, who died in 2012, was the grandson of King Monivong. King Norodom Sihanouk ruled Cambodia twice as king. The first reign was from 1941 to 1955 with real power and the second reign was from 1993 to 2004 as a ceremonial role." (*A History of Cambodia*, fourth edition. David Chandler, Silkworm Books, p.119)

Around that time, some elites of Cambodia went to study abroad returned as communists. After their return, those elites rose to power as the Khmer Rouge (communists of Cambodia). They eventually killed Prime Minister Lon Nol (the person who was in authority with the support of the United States) and invaded Phnom Penh. The Khmer Rouge desired to build an ideal nation based on farming after massacring countless intellectuals and doctors. They had an anti-Vietnam policy and slaughtered innumerable Vietnamese who were living to preserve the lands they had received from their ancestors. The Killing Fields that is located outside of the city is living proof of the history of this brutal genocide during Pol Pot's (leader of Khmer Rouge) regime. Vietnam's invasion in 1979 started a long and drawn-out 20-year civil war in Cambodia. This civil war was ended by the Paris Agreement in 1993 and Cambodia finally found peace. Cambodia and Vietnam have been hated enemies for a long time. Their relationship is like Korea and Japan. Vietnamese people in Cambodia do not have Cambodian citizenship even after many generations. They do not have Vietnamese citizenship either.

Today, Cambodia has been under the dictatorship of Hun Sen for over 30 years. Recently he forcefully dissolved opposition parties that were very crucial in Cambodia. He also turned his back against America and became pro-China. Cambodia has been facing economic difficulty with paying back money that they borrowed from China. However, Hun Sen has still been stubborn with his dictatorship.

EXPERIENCING CAMBODIAN CULTURE

Transportation

When I arrived in Cambodia in 2004, there were not many cars and the roads were in poor condition. Four-wheel-drive cars symbolized wealth. For working-class people, the major modes of transportation were moto (motorcycle), tuk-tuks (two-wheeled motorbike carriages) and used bongo vans (used to go to the countryside). Taxis were available in inner-cities. And when you needed to make a quick trip to the countryside, bullet taxis (used Toyota Camrys) were available.

Tuk-tuks, carriages linked to motorcycles, are a much loved transportation option by travelers in Cambodia. The fees for tuk-tuk rental were at that time approximately $15 USD for a whole day and $7 USD for a half day. Small motorcycles called Motos are very fast, which saves a lot of time, but a little too fast and furious for my taste, and made me dizzy just watching them zoom by. If you are a traveler in Phnom Penh, you will see many fast-moving mottos that dangerously carry 4-5 people on one bike. This illustrates why Cambodia is number one in the world for traffic accidents. However, this gives you a feel for the dynamics of life in the city. Today, there is an increased number of used cars on better paved and clean roads. In Cambodia almost 90% of cars are used Toyotas. Pollution, however, is now a serious issue. In 2018, many parts of Phnom Penh were under construction for road expansion. I remember distinctly, as I was on my way to the airport to head back to the States for good, how bad the traffic jam was.

PART 2

Towards
Cambodia

" Therefore, my dear friends, as you have
always obeyed—not only in my presence,
but now much more in my absence—continue to work out your salvation with fear
and trembling, for it is God who works in
you to will and to act in order to fulfill his
good purpose (Philippians 2:12-13, NIV).

4

Vision Trip 2004

Vision Trip to Cambodia

On January 2004, I went on a 10-day vision trip to Cambodia. It was more like a pre-missions trip to get a glimpse of our upcoming full-time missions life. This trip was led by World Concern and Ron Lamb, a former president of CDS. Through this trip God led me to 4 missionaries who were already on the field and the dental director of the Ministry of Health. This meeting with them heavily influenced most of the decisions that were made for my long-term missions. In this chapter, I would like to share about my relationships with these 5 people.

Meeting with Wilem Van Dis, the Director of ICC

Since my desire was to teach dentistry at Cambodia National Dental School, I decided to interview Wilem Van Dis, a missionary and director of ICC (International Cooperation Cambodia). Dentals schools were aided by ICC's European department of Missions. Wilem is Dutch and was in charge of the dental school as a director of ICC. As I was talking with him about teaching at dental schools, I learned that he wasn't on good terms with a certain Korean missionary. Wilem shared his hurtful experience with this Korean missionary. He expressed displeasure with one particular Korean missionary who was focusing on taking away members from his church instead of cooperating as missionaries to build God's kingdom. I could see that for a long time he was not able to resolve his anger towards the Korean missionary. Furthermore, his grudge, caused by one Korean missionary's mistake, was affecting my ministry.

Wilem shared this hurtful experience with me. A few years prior, the Korean missionary started a church near by the ICC church pastored by Wilem Van Dis. The Korean missionary started to give free rice to the residents around his church. So some of ICC church members moved to Korean missionary's church. At that moment, Wilem was angry to see how the Korean missionary was focusing on taking away members from his church instead of cooperating as missionaries to build God's kingdom. That negative impression had deeply affected Wilem and led him to have a closed mind towards all Koreans. Wilem believed that all Korean missionaries were greedy and competitive, interested only in increasing their numbers by taking people from other churches.

Wilem's unrecovered hurt was so clearly visible when I introduced myself as a Korean American. Wilem was so close minded to me just because I was a first-generation Korean. In the end, I could not get into the ICC missions department. To be honest, I was more embarrassed and ashamed that Wilem had to experience such a thing, than anything. The bigger problem is that such a shameful thing happens quite frequently. What missionary Wilem experienced is unfortunately representative of what happens in many Korean churches. I believe Korean churches need to stop sending out missionaries merely out of competition. Churches need to professionally and thoroughly train every missionary. Even before the training starts, churches need to carefully examine the character and life of their missionary candidates. After I returned from my vision trip, I received an official rejection letter from Wilem Van Dis. In his letter, Wilem suggested, "It would be great if you worked at a missional dental clinic in a mission hospital treating people in poverty."

One missionary's ungodly acts had not only stumbled another missionary but also taken away a ministry opportunity that I deeply desired. Words cannot express my shock and disappointment after receiving the rejection letter. The despair I felt from the rejection after 10 years of preparation was very intense.

Mr. and Mrs. Choo, a Missionary Couple from OMF

The relationship I developed with Dr. Chern Chern Choo and Dr. Yewon Choo (both Chinese Malaysians) became a crucial connection God allowed us to have during our missions to Cambodia. This couple faithfully teamed with me and my wife to serve Cambodia together.

Mr. Choo and family

Mrs. Choo, while doing ministry with her husband in Cambodia for 10 years, went to Singapore and obtained a master's degree of orthodontics in 3 years. When she came back to Cambodia, she began teaching Orthodontics at the graduate school of the only National Dental College in Cambodia.

Missionary Dukgun Cha and his wife, Hanna Ko, from Wycliff

Mr. Cha was doing translation ministry under Mr. Van Dis. He was working to translate into the language of the Cham Tribe. The Cham tribe, as mentioned earlier, were now Muslims residing near the Mekong River as fishermen. Although they had their own language, they were discriminated against by Cambodians for being a minority group. The Cham tribe were descendants of the Champa Empire. Their main residence is located in the center of Vietnam. For a short period, the Cham tribe had taken and reigned over Angkor Empire. However, as the Vietnamese came down to the south, the Champa Empire fell and the whole tribe came into Cambodia after converting to Islam. Missionary Cha, who moved his ministry location from Phnom Penh to Kampong Chhnang, had recently completed the translation of the New Testament into the Cham language.

Dental Director of Health Department

When I met the dental director of the Health Department in Cambodia I asked him, "How many licensed dentists are there in Cambodia?" He said there were about 320 dentists and 60 of them were male nurses who received the license after only 6 months of training in Vietnam. I was very shocked to hear that. Cambodia urgently needed dentists if there were only 300 to serve a population of 12 million people. Although there were unlicensed, Chinese-Cambodian dentists called Traditional

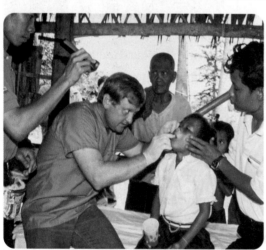

Ron Lamb (current president of World Dental Relief)

Dentists, it was obvious that there was a desperate need for change. These Traditional Dentists were untrained people but somewhat sanctioned. Since there was such a shortage of dentists, the Cambodian government acknowledged them as official dentists

and allowed them to per-
form dental treatments.
The dental law dictated that
a licensed doctor should
oversee these unlicensed
Traditional Dentists once a
month, but nothing like this
was actually happening. The
quality of their treatment, of
course, was very poor.

The five people that I
met in Cambodia during
this 10-day vision trip were

Dr. WM Calnon & Ron Lam (2012 Humanitarian Award)

God-given guides to me and like a compass whenever I had to make
decisions relating to missions. First, through the rejection letter from
Mr. Van Dis of ICC, God led me to minister to the poor through CRM.
Since even the rejection was under God's sovereignty, Mr. Van Dis and
I became partners in God's kingdom. Although my personal desire to
teach at a dental school had not been fulfilled, I could see how God
was faithfully working to raise future dentists through this one and
only dental school in Cambodia: National University of Dentistry. The
National University of Dentistry followed the French education model
requiring a 7-year term in college. However, only 25 students were attending at the time, which meant there was so much potential for the
school to grow.

Meeting with President Yabro from CDS and Ron Lam (current
president of World Dental Relief) had also become a crucial connection in regards to Cambodia missions. World Dental Relief (WDR) is
a missions organization that supports dental missionaries with dental
materials and equipment that have been donated.

"

Until I come, devote yourself to the public reading of Scripture, to preaching and to teaching. Do not neglect your gift, which was given you through prophecy when the body of elders laid their hands on you. Be diligent in these matters; give yourself wholly to them, so that everyone may see your progress. Watch your life and doctrine closely. Persevere in them, because if you do, you will save both yourself and your hearers (1 Timothy 4:13-16, NIV).

5

Ordination and Send-off

Ministry to the Poor through CRM

My vision trip to Cambodia in January 2004 had completely changed my missional direction. The rejection to teach at the dental school from Mr. Van Dis had led me towards ministry to the poor. I will first share how God had already divinely prepared me for dental missions to the poor. Then I'll also share how God divinely led me to one person to start a new ministry.

Before I left for my vision trip to Cambodia, I went to Saint Andrew Abby Monastery to spend quiet time with God. I wanted to have intimate fellowship with God through meditating on the Bible and praying. The morning after I arrived at the monastery, I went to a cafeteria to eat breakfast. There, I got to sit at a table with a missionary named Steve Sharp. He was a missionary from CRM who was taking a sabbatical from poverty-relief missions in Venezuela. I introduced myself to him and told him that I was preparing to go to Cambodia for full-time dental missions. He told me about Sue Lloyd, the executive director of InnerCHANGE (poverty-relief ministry at CRM) and asked me to meet her in person. I got the napkin with the name of the director, slipped it into my pocket and left the monastery. When I came home, I wrote the name and phone number in my notebook but quickly forgot all about it as I was leaving on my vision trip to Cambodia. Then, as I mentioned, when I came back I was devastated by the rejection from Mr. Van Dis.

God is so amazing. My own plan was to teach at a dental school in Cambodia. I never really thought about inner city ministry to the poor, until I talked to professor Watson from Fuller, previously. Even then, I didn't know anyone from the poverty ministry of CRM (InnerCHANGE). However, God was preparing me for this ministry to the poor instead of the teaching ministry at a dental school. How immeasurable His will is! God not only exposed me to CRM ministry through my professor at Fuller, but He also led me to the director of InnerCHANGE through a missionary from Venezuela I happened to sit with at breakfast. It is so amazing how perfect and delicate God's plan is! God is faithful and He never makes mistakes. If we know that every single moment of our lives is under God's sovereignty, we would have to love and serve the people we meet daily.

"Abraham looked up and there in a thicket he saw a ram caught by its horns. He went over and took the ram and sacrificed it as a burnt offering instead of his son. So Abraham called that place The Lord Will Provide. And to this day it is said, "On the mountain of the Lord it will be provided" (Genesis 22:13-14 NIV).

I was exhausted after coming back from my vision trip to Cambodia. Since the plan to teach at a dental school had fallen through, I became very anxious. But, the Holy Spirit led me to think of one person and one organization: Sue Lloyd and CRM. Professor Jude Watson, who first introduced me to CRM, was living in inner-city Los Angeles with her husband. As members of CRM, Prof. Watson and her husband started a

2014 CRM Conference in Cancun, Mexico

church there and lived around Alvarado and Union St. in Los Angeles.

As the Holy Spirit reminded me of Sue Lloyd, the director of CRM InnerCHANGE, I immediately called her and went to visit her. At that time, her office was right next to MacArthur Park on Alvarado and 7th Street. She advised me to be sent off as an official CRM InnerCHANGE missionary to Cambodia. There were four departments within CRM: International Missions, Domestic Missions, Poverty Missions (Inner-CHANGE), Business Missions (Business as Missions). Sue advised me four years term as regular missionary, but I thought four years were too long. So I became part of the poverty mission and committed 2 years as an intern.

Ordination at CRM

Finally my wife and I had begun our last stage of preparation for full-time missions to Cambodia. In July 2004, we went to San Francisco to receive a 2-week-long InnerCHANGE training. Towards the end of July, my wife and I were gloriously ordained as missionaries to Cambodia. GDA (a Korean-American dental missions organization) prepared a grand send-off service at Berendo Street Baptist Church. GDA passionately supported us and even came to Cambodia 3 times for portable dental missions. I give glory to God and thanks to all the members of GDA.

Send-off to Cambodia

On August 6, 2004, Tina and I arrived at Phnom Penh, Cambodia. We were sent off by CRM for two years as interns for InnerCHANGE. As soon as we got off the plane, we were greeted with an intense humidity. It was like a premonition, a foreboding message to us that the road ahead was not going to be easy. But at that moment, rain started to pour and it became very cool. In chapter 6, I will share about Mark Smith (team leader of InnerCHANGE) and Dave Everitt and how God led us to build a dentistry clinic within the Southern Baptist Mission Hospital.

EXPERIENCING CAMBODIAN CULTURE

Prahok

Prahok (Cambodian-style salted fish) is a traditional dish of Cambodia. It is very similar to salted fish from South Korea. Freshwater fish is marinated and fermented with salt. Cambodians usually don't like the fish from the sea since the smell of it is very strong.The only fish they eat from the oceans is sea bream. Small fish caught in the rice field or river are fermented in salt and used as ingredients in various traditional dishes of Cambodia. There are many varieties of prahok as much as there are many varieties of fish in Cambodia. Cambodians really enjoy prahok.

Koreans usually use shrimp, largehead hairtail, sardines or various kinds of sea fish or their eggs. For Cambodians, it would be very new and strange to make prahok with sea fish. My wife and I also enjoyed eating cockles caught from the mud flat of the southern sea. They tasted exactly the same as the ones in South Korea.

PART 3

In Cambodia

"

And even if our gospel is veiled, it is veiled to those who are perishing. The god of this age has blinded the minds of unbelievers, so that they cannot see the light of the gospel that displays the glory of Christ, who is the image of God. For what we preach is not ourselves, but Jesus Christ as Lord, and ourselves as your servants for Jesus' sake (2 Corinthians 4:3-5, NIV).

6

Ministry to the Poor
(Dental Clinic in Hospital)

Dentistry at the Southern Baptist Mission Dental Clinic

When we arrived to Phnom Penh Airport on August 6, 2004, Mark Smith, the team leader, welcomed us warmly. He took us to a hotel near the king's palace where we stayed for one month. There was a huge temple near our hotel and every early morning, the Buddhist prayer was played through a loudspeaker. I remember I was not able to sleep well because of it, but it was interesting to experience.

InnerCHANGE Ministry had weekly meetings on Wednesdays at 4pm. The meeting was for the missionaries to report ministry status and prayer requests to pray together. We attended our first meeting and introduced ourselves to the team. We rented a place across Dave Everitt's house. We met Touch, the landlord's aunt and younger sister (Leng Chan Heng). Leng Chan Heng is also one of the important encounters I had in Cambodia.

Every Sunday morning, my wife and I attended a local church. Then, we went to ICF (International Christian Fellowship) at 4pm to have another worship service with other missionaries. With the help of an assistant pastor, who was our neighbor, I shared the gospel with Touch (which means small) and she accepted Christ. Touch was my first fruit in Cambodia. That seed of the gospel was passed to Leng Chan Heng and Heng also accepted Christ. After she committed her life to Jesus, she wholeheartedly helped my ministry. Touch's son Mann, who lived in the countryside, also came and accepted Jesus.

With the recommendation of Mark Smith and Dave Everitt, I was assigned to open dental department at CSI (Cooperative Services International) mission hospital. CSI is an NGO of Southern Baptist.

Dave Everitt was one of founding members of this hospital along with Southern Baptist missionaries. The Preah Ketmealea Military hospital (Army, Navy, Air Force combined) gave CSI a building, a former patient ward, inside the hospital compound. The 2-story building was large enough for medical departments downstairs and storage upstairs.

Dr. Kendrick Kahler, MD, hospital director, allowed me to set up a dental department on the 2nd floor. The 2nd floor was large enough for a dental clinic and lab.

The military hospital has their own dental department with 5 dentists officers and Lt. Colonel department head.

One thing was good: CSI did not have to pay rent and the electricity bill.

Ordination and Raising Support at CDS

Tina and I had set a goal to raise $30,000 to build one dental office. In order to get ordained and raise support, we went back to the States. As we were staying in the States for 3 months, we were ordained once more in Orlando, Florida, at the general assembly of CDS. The president during that year was Jody Yabro. As we were getting ordained at the general assembly, my wife and I deeply experienced God's grace and glory. As Paul told Timothy, "Do not neglect your gift, which was given you through prophecy when the body of elders laid their hands on you. Be diligent in these matters; give yourself wholly to them, so that everyone may see your progress" (1 Timothy 4:14-15, NIV). The ordination service was a time for me to experience God's favor. My wife also officially became a missionary of CDS through ordination. When we were on the missions field, we would often think about God's anointing we experienced in ordination, and Dr. Jody Yabro's advice "that

I was ordained by CDS as a missionary to Cambodia

everyone may see your progress" (1 Timothy 4:15, NIV) whenever we faced hardships. Yabro's encouragement renewed our passion and calling for Cambodia every day.

"However, I consider my life worth nothing to me; my only aim is to finish the race and complete the task the Lord Jesus has given me—the task of testifying to the good news of God's grace" (Acts 20:24, NIV).

At the ordination, my wife and I teared up so much thinking about God's grace to such undeserving people like us.

After the ordination, we asked the headquarters if we could raise financial support from the members of the local CDS. Thankfully we received $15,000 from the headquarters and we were asked to raise another $15,000 on our own. Some members committed to give a monthly offering and some gave one-time gifts.

There were 4 churches and members of GDA that also supported us financially. There were some individual supporters as well. I asked for monthly support and told someone I actually need two dental chairs rather than one. Deacon Sungho Kim (Westminster Presbyterian Church, president of an optical parts company) from my home church offered money that was enough to buy a dental chair. At the end, my wife and I were able to raise $50,000, which was enough to build 2 treatment rooms. We gladly returned to Cambodia in December 2004.

Grand Opening of Dental Department at CSI Hospital

In order to get a dentist license and work as a doctor in Cambodia, you need an American dental license, diploma from dental school, and a membership card from ADA (American Dental Association). As soon as you submit these 3 documents, the dental license will be issued by the government. If you have a plan to go on dental missions to a third -world country, it is very important that you become a member of ADA. If you get a recommendation letter from your missions organization, the fee for membership registration at ADA will be waived.

After 4 months of preparation at the CSI dental clinic near the king's palace in Phnom Penh, we finally completed work setting up our dental office. On May 4, 2005, the clinic was officially open to the public. The staff members of the clinic were my wife, Dr. Sokha as an intern, Luon

Rachana as a receptionist, two assistants (Sophen and Chan), and the janitor Bongtom. One year later, Sovanny and Leng Chan Heng joined as assistants.

Many people working in the dental field came for the grand opening service. Mark Smith was in charge of the sermon and the congratulatory message was done by Pastor Peter Kong (president of the Korean Missionary Association in Cambodia).

Dental staff at the grand opening of the dental clinic on May 4, 2005

Our daily routine always started at 6 a.m. with Khmer language study. Mr. Kong (a Cambodian) came to our house and tutored us for one hour. All foreign missionaries in Cambodia usually focus on learning the Khmer language during the first year. After the first year, you were allowed to do ministry work along with your language study. However, dental ministry to the poor was so urgent, I was asked to start ministry immediately. That is why we had to wake up early in the morning to study the local language. One mistake I made when studying the language was focusing on formal language instead of conversational language. I was too anxious to teach the Bible to the local people. However, ordinary Cambodians used easy language, so formal language was not as helpful for teaching the Bible. After our language class, we went to the dental clinic by 7:30 a.m. and spent devotional time with God for 30 minutes. Then, from 8 a.m. to 5 p.m. we worked fully and took care of our patients. The patients were mainly poor Cambodian patients whom missionaries brought. We also treated Korean missionaries, OMF missionaries, various members of mission organization, and local pastors with their families. Poverty-stricken families from the area, as well as the military and their families also came to our clinic.

Our dental clinic was always busy. During the busy time, our intern Sokha Meas decided to move to another dental clinic that would pay him better. Later, he introduced his friend Makara as an intern in August 2005. Makara was not a believer, so I consistently prayed for him and showed him love. Finally he opened his heart and accepted the gospel message. He was also baptized and became a faithful believer. Today, he runs the dental clinic called ADC (American Dental Clinic) that my wife and I started. Although the dental clinic was in need of a new intern for quite a while, God's plan was to save Makara, who eventually came as our new intern. When it was time for me to leave Cambodia for good, Makara's parting words touched me deeply, "I didn't understand why Mr. Cho left the comfortable life in America and came to Cambodia. I thought there was something fishy about him coming here. However, I was moved by his genuine love for Cambodians and wanted to believe in Jesus." I was deeply moved and comforted by his words.

One sad thing that happened was he reluctantly married a non-Christian wife. I strongly encouraged him to marry a Christian woman, but it seemed he couldn't disobey his parents and break off his engagement. As his faith in Jesus was deepening, he kept postponing his wedding. He didn't want to marry an unbelieving, stubborn fiancée. One day, his fiancée's father, tired of waiting, told him that their families will become enemies if they don't get married that coming Saturday. Makara couldn't postpone the wedding anymore. He told us one week before the wedding day that he was getting married. Wedding ceremonies in Cambodia are usually very grand. The bride and the groom-to-be usually sent out invitations one month before the ceremony. However, Makara didn't even have time to pass out invitations.

Makara and his wife have two beautiful daughters, but his wife is still not a believer. Makara's wife grumbles to her husband about not being able to place a Buddhist statue at home. Makara has been having a hard time resisting his wife's request. One time, the wife said the reason for their first daughter's dengue fever was not having the Buddhist statue at home. She sarcastically said, "If you pray to your God and our daughter gets better, I will believe in Him."

"And even if our gospel is veiled, it is veiled to those who are perishing. The god of this age has blinded the minds of unbelievers, so that they cannot see the light of the gospel that displays the glory of Christ, who is the image of God" (2 Corinthians 4:3-4, NIV).

I pray earnestly that the power of Jesus's death and resurrection will come upon the house of Makara and bring his wife to accept Jesus.

Busy Ministry at the Dental Clinic

Here is a glimpse into what the daily operations looked like at our dental clinic:

Dental ministry to the poor and under-privileged

1) Patients were introduced to us through referrals from missionaries. When they came to the dental clinic, they would receive a dental test on the first floor. Only the patients with problems were then sent to the clinic on the second floor.

2) The patients who were sent to the clinic would then start treatment.

3) Dental expenses were paid both by the patients and the missionary who referred them. There was no free treatment. Patients were supposed to pay at least a dollar so they would feel self-reliant. However, since the missionaries were responsible for the expenses, they had a hard time paying for expensive treatments that required dental lab work.

4) Sometimes patients who came with missionaries were allowed to skip the testing procedure on the first floor and came straight to the clinic especially when they already had symptoms.

5) Those who I knew personally, missionaries who took care of Vietnamese, local pastors and patients that came through missionaries received extra care and benefits.

6) Foreign missionaries including Koreans always paid for the treatments.

7) A few Chinese heard about us and came to get treatments as well.

8) Many OMF missionaries came to our clinic to get treatments since the care from local dentists was not of high quality. Dr. Choo of OMF also strongly encouraged the missionaries to come to our clinic.

9) It is not an exaggeration to say more than half of the Cambodian population had teeth problems. Not having patients was never an issue for us at any time. The problem was always not having enough resources and staff to help them all.

As we did treatments inside the clinic, the gospel was presented to the people waiting outside. Our mission team always did their best to run the clinic and share the gospel at the same time. Bong Tom, who was very eloquent in speech, presented the gospel message clearly to the people. God blessed her to see many of them accept Jesus. It was also very common to see dental students coming to our clinic to learn on the field. Our clinic was a perfect place for them to gain field experience.

As a pre-missionary, 2 years of internship passed by very quickly. After two years of internship, my wife and I returned to the States to become long-term missionaries. Because we were able to start the clinic in Cambodia, we were convicted of God's plan to continue our dental missions. When my wife and I returned to the States on August 2006, we passed the Birkman test together and were sent off again as long-term missionaries (2006-2017). With overflowing hope and dreams, we went back to Cambodia. During our temporary leave, Dr. Makara had done an excellent job running the clinic.

Establishment of Dental Laboratory

As we were managing the dental clinic, we were in desperate need of a dental lab. Since the techniques available in Cambodia were poor, we had to take new dental impressions frequently. Partial dentures were especially hard to get. Cambodia followed the European model whereas I followed the American one. Cambodian labs had never seen the American model, so my partial denture design was very new to them. This created many difficulties in making necessary components, so we established a dental lab of our own in 2006.

At that time, we contacted Pastor Bong Ki Cho from Cambodia Presbyterian Theological Institute to ask for help. He connected us to a deacon named William Hur from Cerritos Presbyterian Church. Deacon Hur had a

William Hur is teaching techniques to the dental laboratory staff.

heart for missions and a vision to train young Combodians to become dental technicians. Deacon Hur came to Cambodia for short-term missions and went on portable dental missions to Kampong Chnang, Pastor Bonki Cho's church. Deacon Hur made temporary dentures called Stay Plates for the patients. Then, he returned to the States with a promise that he would come back to Cambodia. After 6 months, deacon Hur returned with his wife, Youngja Hur, and their middle-school -aged son. His daughter Michelle already graduated from college and was working, so she was not able to come.

I reached out to all my supporters and the members of CDS letting them know we needed $28,000 to build a dental lab. Our faithful God sent exactly $28,000 through them and made it possible for William to build a dental lab. William served faithfully in Cambodia for 4 years. Then, in 2011, he had to return to the States since the international school that allowed his son to apply for colleges in America was too expensive. I had to take over running the lab temporarily and eventually transferred the job to a German missionary named Evan Tardic. When Evan Tardic left Cambodia, I took over again and eventually transferred the job to William's apprentices. Their names were Sovan Kol, Samphors and Vuth.

Let me share more about William Hur. When William returned to San Diego, he was diagnosed with cancer called cholangiocarcinoma (bile duct cancer) two years later. He eventually went to be with the Lord. He was only 55 years old. It was such a heartbreaking experience for me. He took out a $100,000 loan from his home equity to use for missions. Then, the real estate market dropped dramatically in 2008. William suffered a lot from the market drop, and he lost his home, but he still trusted God and depended on Him. When I heard about his passing, I was in the States during my sabbatical month to attend CDS meeting. I cried as I was reading a tribute at William's funeral. A great soldier of God had completed his mission and went to be with the Lord. Many people who came to the funeral remembered him and honored his commitment for God. Pastor Steve Hall, the director of the missions department at CRM Business as Mission and Jim Caya, a member of the missions department came to mourn. Pastor Hall later expressed concern whether I would be able to finish the memorial tribute because he saw that I was unable to calm the overwhelming emotions and feelings that I was experiencing. Missionary Willam Hur lived a life that showed what it means to be a wise steward of God. William's daughter also got into a pharmacy school as she was working full time. I remember how happy William was when he heard his daughter got into pharmacy school. He passed away not long after he heard the news.

As I was coming back to Cambodia, I was very focused on the need to develop our ability to deliver portable dental treatment. I bought 2 portable dental units from a company called Asepticos and 2 patient chairs. I will explain more in detail about portable dental missions in chapter 7.

EXPERIENCING CAMBODIAN CULTURE

Tradition of Matriarchal Society

As mentioned previously, Cambodia is a matriarchal society. All the parents' wealth is passed down to the daughters. When a son gets married, he goes to live with the wife's side of the family to farm. Today, many young men live in the cities, so they only spend around 6 months living with the in-laws outside of the city, and then come back. Oldest daughters in the family usually work at sewing companies or do business to support the family and often miss the opportunity to get married. Many of them just live as singles. Cambodian society expects the oldest daughters to pay for the schooling of their siblings as well as support the parents financially. It is a harsh obligation given by the society to their women. Parents usually have a very small piece of land to farm. Many of them will end up losing even that small land and live in poverty. Again, this burden falls on the oldest daughters to take care of them. That is the reason for the increasing number of single women in Cambodia. In our own community, there were 4 single women. Even if a woman is married, she is mainly responsible for the family finances and runs the business. The husbands are in the position of helper to their wives. However, men are solely responsible for matters of the military and politics.

Frank and Tina Cho attending a traditional Cambodian wedding

> Now may the God of peace, who through the blood of the eternal covenant brought back from the dead our Lord Jesus, that great Shepherd of the sheep, equip you with everything good for doing his will, and may he work in us what is pleasing to him, through Jesus Christ, to whom be glory for ever and ever. Amen (Hebrews 13:20-21, NIV).

7

Portable Dental Missions

Portable dental missions was important and urgently needed in Cambodia. Cambodians love their sweets, but they didn't have the practice of brushing their teeth. The cavity rate was very high. It was also rare to find any dental clinics, which led to almost everyone having cavities. Wherever we went out to do portable dental work, there was always a shortage of workers. There would be massive overflows of patients coming to our portable dental clinics every time. Whenever we went on portable missions, medical doctors along with dentists went together. The bus that we took was like a medical center. Our portable dental clinic were able to help patients with all kinds of dental conditions. Portable dental clinic were done 6 times every year (3 near Phnom Penh, 3 far from the city).

Introducing Portable Dental Clinic Ministry

Usually portable medical and dental ministry was a stepping stone for many missionaries from all over the world to plant churches. However, without the help of the public workers, neither portable dental clinic missions nor church planting was possible. That is why we tried very hard to maintain good relationships with the public workers. The following are tips for effective portable dental clinic ministry.

First, we prioritized the treatment of the public workers whenever there was a need. It was a necessity as a foreign missionary to have a harmonious relationship with the local public worker to maintain security and do effective evangelism.

In terms of treating patients, we prioritized cavity treatment over teeth extraction and removal. This was to prevent future teeth extraction. If you only extract teeth without cavity treatment, the cavity grows and you end up extracting another tooth next time. It's like a bottomless pit. Continuous teeth extraction is not a helpful treatment. Although we needed a lot of tools, time, and electricity to treat cavities, cavity treatment and teeth filling were better ways to protect other healthy teeth. Also, it was the best way to reduce the number of patients coming to the clinic in the long term.

We also educated patients about oral health. The education included how to brush your teeth or floss. Free toothbrushes were handed out. Floss, however, was not available for the people living in the countryside, so we told the patients to use two strands of thread from home. As one team of missionaries was treating patients, another team shared the gospel of Jesus. We as a team effectively and passionately shared the gospel in and out of season.

Second, portable medical/dental missions is an excellent tool for pioneering missionaries to grab the attention of the local people and invite them. Our portable dental ministry team was always divided into two parts: dental treatment and evangelism. We also gave the list of people who accepted Jesus to the local missionaries or pastors to follow up. Then, the new believers could receive personal care and training.

Third, we also accepted requests from local pastors (through EFC meetings) to come to their churches and run portable dental clinic. Running portable dental clinic had helped many local churches to reach out to many people.

Prison Ministry

Missionary Heap Him, one of our team members, did ministry to the disabled as well as prison ministry. He started PBLS (Peace Builder Life Skills) program which was specifically designed for inmates to build character, and has been very faithful with the ministry until today. The program was created with the intention of helping the inmates find inner peace through learning about God's love. One visible outcome of the program was a decrease in the number of fights within the prison.

At that time, one of the sons of a pastor (leader of a Baptist denomination in Cambodia) was imprisoned at Kampong Cham Prison. The pastor's name was Kakada Tuon. Our team went for dental ministry to Kampong Cham Prison 3 times to help the pastor's son. As we were treating the staff members and the inmates, we were also able to share the gospel with them. We also visited Sunrise AIDS Hospice, a place where Diane Moss was serving. Diane Moss was a missionary in charge of hospice ministry for the inmates and tuberculosis patients. The hospice we visited was specifically for tuberculosis patients. By the request of the hospice, we visited another prison in the city and did dental missions there. Upon the request of Dr. Callum Durward, the Dean of International University School of Dentistry, we joined his prison ministry (One-2-One Cambodia).

Ministry of Diane Moss (Director of AIDS & Hospice Ministry)

In 2001, Sunrise AIDS Hospice was first established as Inner-CHANGE of CRM's affiliated organization. The organization was built to help AIDS patients and provide hospice care. Diane Moss, the director, started this ministry with home-based care (caring for civilians). Then, after two years in 2003, she started a hospice ministry at Kampong Cham City. Many mission organizations including OMF supported Diane's AIDS and hospice ministry with sending missionaries to help and prayer. Tuberculosis patients were treated through home visitations. AIDS patients were quarantined at an assigned location. At that time, 15% of the whole population of Cambodia was HIV positive and they were dying from getting infected. Diane visited the homes of patients, did treatment and provided medications for AIDS patients. For final-stage AIDS patients she brought them to a large facility for hospice. Every year Sunrise Ministry budgeted $100,000 to help fight the AIDS epidemic. There was a group of supporters back in America that supported the ministry until 2016. During that time, Diane Moss left for Romania as a team leader, and Susan Smith became the new leader for Sunrise Ministry. Although the support from the States had ended in 2016, Mark and Susan never stopped raising support and continued the hospice ministry. The hospice was mainly filled with AIDS patients. Until today, Sunrise is making great efforts to eliminate AIDS and tuberculosis in Cambodia. Now, with the help of the UN and several NGOs, the percentage of AIDS patients has been reduced to about 0.5 percent of the total population, but tuberculosis still remains as a major disease that cannot be treated in Cambodia.

Whenever I think of Diane Moss, I can never forget about my encounter with a young orphan boy. I even wrote an essay on my special memory with the boy under the section "The Jesus I Met".

"The Jesus I Met"

Diane Moss (Director of Sunrise AIDS, Tuberculosis Hospice Institution) was helping a government-run orphanage. One day she invited our dental team to come and do dental treatments.

We arrived at an orphanage in Kampong Cham with a dental mission team (directed by Dr. Jeong-gyu Choi) from South Korea. We moved the equipment from the car to the indoor auditorium, and the orphans were helping the team by carrying some of the small items. At that time, I noticed a boy, seemingly 10 years old, carrying the medication boxes. The boy was exceptionally short compared to the other children around him. Then, I began to hand out tickets to the patients to determine their wait order. The boy who was helping the team earlier received ticket #10. We treated the members of the orphanage all day long. Because the staff members of the orphanage brought neighbors on top of the orphans, the treatment didn't end even after 5 p.m. I endured terrible pain in my back that day but we continued taking care of the patients.

"The boy I met" who eagerly carries medicine boxes

As I was about to get up after work, a female employee brought a boy. It was the short boy that helped the mission team carry the equipment and received ticket #10. I asked the employee why the boy couldn't receive the treatment earlier if his number was 10? The boy was deaf and he couldn't hear his number. Even with the extreme pain in my back, I settled back in my chair to examine the boy's mouth. Yellow calculus was covering all over the child's teeth. Surprisingly and thankfully, there were no cavities. Although it took some time, I carefully removed all the hard calculus. I also taught him how to brush his teeth. It was late at night by the time our team was leaving. Even though I was extremely exhausted, my heart was overjoyed as I thought of that boy. The boy, who was very short and had hearing problems. The kind boy who was so willing to help our team move our stuff. The boy who couldn't receive treatment until the end. I believe he was Jesus who came to me in disguise. Thinking about the boy made my heart compassionate. So, I was able to return home with overflowing joy.

Ministry of Dave Everitt at Mondulkiri Province

Mondulkiri's Oraeyang village, where Dave Everitt (a member of our team) was working, was the first remote area that our portable dental

Truck that fell into a muddy road

clinic team visited. I had to drive all day to get there. The road was unpaved. The truck loaded with equipment fell into a muddy pit, and a 4-wheel -drive car had to come pull our truck out. In the southern Sihanouk region, the road conditions were pretty good, but the eastern Koh Kong region was rough. There were no bridges. so we had to take the ferry twice to move all the ministry team members, along with the equipment and our truck, across the two rivers.

We had to cross a big river with everyone on board. Now the bridge has been completed and you can move around a lot faster. It's a whole different world now.

Siem Pang Ministry (Missionary Annette, Bunchan, and Scott)

When I first went to Siem Pang, I had to go with all my luggage from the capital city of Stung Treng. My wife and I stayed at Stung Treng overnight and loaded the luggage into a ship early the next morning. Tina and all the team members would leave Stung Treng, taking a boat slowly up the Se Kong River, and arriving to Siem Pang around noon. The doctors from the United States and I would arrive from Stung Treng the next day taking a speedboat. The Se Kong River to Siem Pang was very beautiful. When returning from our portable dental ministry, the US mission team and I would return first again by

Portable dental ministry team crossing the Mekong River by ferry

speedboat, and the rest of the team took a wooden boat that took 3 hours. The second time we went to Siem Pang, the dirt road was open and our team was able to drive a dental treatment vehicle. This took about 12 hours and it was a very tough journey. The road is a lot better today, though it is still a dirt road.

Our last visit to Siem Pang was in 2017. At that time, Mrs. Kilen Yamauchi, who had permanently returned to Cambodia from the US, gave me $600 to distribute 70 bags of rice to poor families. So I asked missionary Philip (Cambodia regional director of YWAM, England) to use the $600 for ministry to the poor. However, Philip thought about it and refused to receive the $600. The reason for his refusal was that with $600 he could only give rice to some people. This advice was given to him from an experienced ministry worker.

Kilen Yamauchi was a Cambodian who evangelized to people very powerfully. She worked as a head nurse in an oral surgery dental office in San Francisco. She always led many people to the Lord through Holy Spirit-filled evangelism. Kilen first heard about me from

Kilen Yamauchi sharing the gospel powerfully

her friend who knows medical Dr. Modec at CSI hospital. She heard that there was a Korean dentist who was in Cambodia doing missions. She learned more about me through the videos on the CRM website and after reading about why I came to Cambodia she became determined to work with me.

I also went to Siem Pang of Stung Treng Province, where Annette, a single missionary from YWAM England was doing ministry. It was a village in northern Cambodia and on the border of Laos. It was a village that was surrounded by the mountains. People of that region

Missionary Annette Jandrell

had pale skin with large eyes. These people were an ethnic minority within Cambodia. YWAM was working with a local employee to convert river water into drinking water. Annette was planting a church there and taking care of the water ministry. She lived there for eight years without running electrical power, only a small generator. Recently, we received news from Annette that she married a former missionary from YWAM in 2019 and is living happily on the Isle of Man in England.

Pastor Bun Chan, who was working with Annette, was a carpenter, caring for the Siem Pang Church and 7 house churches within the mountain area. Since he was a carpenter, he helped with constructing the church greatly. YWAM does not build church buildings because they let the local people build on their own. Therefore, it took 3 years for Pastor Bun Chan to complete building a small church in Siem Pang. Before we returned home from our portable medical/dental missions, we invited all members of the church to a celebration. In my last portable medical/dental mission trip, I heard some unfortunate news. Pastor Bun Chan was a truly precious shepherd.

The last time we saw him was our third portable dental mission trip in Siem Pang. After our clinic on the first day of the week, I asked the elder of the church, "I don't see Pastor Bun Chan today. What happened?" I was told that Pastor Bun Chan couldn't come because he couldn't see well. I decided to end our work one day early and visited Pastor Bun Chan's house with my wife, Tina. Pastor Chan's house was a traditionally built thatched house that looked like it was about to collapse soon. The house was tilted a little to the side and the floor creaked. The pastor's condition was very bad, to the point that I could hardly recognize him. He became so sick only after 12 years working as a minister.

Pastor Bun Chan and his wife living in such
poor living conditions shocked me greatly.
He was almost blind and it was already too
late for him to get surgery. Because of the
intense sunlight in Cambodia, Pastor Bun
Chan's eyes started getting very cloudy and
he became virtually blind. However, Pastor
Bun Chan said he was still grateful that he
could still see a glimpse of this beautiful
world. We brought Pastor Bun Chan to our

Pastor Bun Chan with Tina

medical/dental clinic the next morning and did medical treatments for
him as our first patient of the day.

Pastor Bun Chan reminded me of Jesus Christ, who came to this
earth as a true shepherd. Like Jesus, Pastor Bun Chan, as a carpenter,
built a beautiful, two-story church with his congregation. However, he
was living in a shabby house. As a true shepherd without greed or self-
ishness, Pastor Chan genuinely practiced the love of Jesus.

Lastly, I would like to introduce missionary Philip.

Missionary Annette had first introduced us to Philip Scott, so whenever I remember missionary Annette, I also recall missionary Philip
Scott, who was missionary Annette's director. He was a veteran missionary who came to Cambodia while the civil war was still going in
1992. That year was when the remnants of the Khmer Rouge were still
out there with guns. The road in Siem Pang at that time was still not
open, so Philip and I had to take a light aircraft to make a visitation
before missions. After my 2nd mobile outreach trip to Siem Pang, I
asked Annette if she could recommend one good Christian high school
graduate for a dental school scholarship. At that time there were no
licensed dentists in the whole province, only the traditional dentists.

Annette recommended the son of a woman elder from her church.
Suon Sambo came down from Phnom Penh and lived on the floor

Missionary Philip (Cambodia Director of YWAM, England)

above the American Dental Clinic, watching the clinic as night security for 7 years. Sambo graduated National Dental School successfully. I trained him for 2 years in ADC, then he opened his own dental clinic with missionary Scott's help.

Philip, along with a medical missionary from Korea he knew well, helped Sambo start a clinic in Stung Treng.

Philip and his team usually focused solely on their ministry in Stung Treng. We worked together very often. The first time that our portable dental clinic went to Siem Pang was an answer to one and a half years of fervent prayer by our receptionist, Rachana. Siem Pang was Rachana's hometown and she knew that the people were desperate for treatment from the medical/dental team. Rachana reached out to missionary Annette for help. As a result, missionary Philip, the YWAM director, and I went to visit Siem Pang. This proved to be very difficult as it took a total of 4 days to get there and back. Also, it was impossible for us to get there by car at that time of year. We had to wait until the water level of the river to rise in order to take a boat there. The second time our portable dental clinic went to Siem Pang took over 12 hours by bus because the dirt road had cracked open. But we were able to keep the promise that we made to Rachana by providing denture treatment to patients in her hometown that would have been unable to access those treatments otherwise.

Ly Chhay and Navy Chann Mission Ministry

First, I would like to introduce the family of Navy Chann, missionaries from Canada. The Navy family were Cambodian refugees who immigrated to Canada and later returned to their home country as missionaries. They were working hard as missionaries in Sre Ambel, located in the northern part of Koh Kong Province in western Cambodia for over 20 years. This was the place where missionary Ly Chhay was born and raised. They always hoped a portable dental team would come. Our team went to Sre Ambel 4 times. Ly and Navy made appointments for the morning and afternoon in each village before the team arrived.

Portable dental clinic team crossing the river by ferry

Navy & Ly, missionaries from Canada

Patients were required to deposit 10 cents to make an appointment. Another one of the ministries they pioneered was when they purchased farmland to create a model farm to teach new farming techniques to the local farmers. They also planted churches in the region. Our church mission team also visited in 2013. The daughter of missionary Navy married a member of the royal family, so Tina and I were also invited to see the royal wedding.

Korean Women Missionaries in Cambodia

I want to take a moment to remember some of the ministry and partnerships we had with a few women missionaries.

In addition to Diane Moss and Annette, there are a few unforgettable women missionaries who were Korean. We had a special annual Christmas dinner for specifically single missionaries. We served them with delicious food at a nice restaurant by Mekong River to recognize their hard work and encourage them. When we first arrived in Cambodia in August 2004, the first thing that caught our attention was the work of female single missionaries and their efforts. On the day we joined the Korean Missionary Society in Cambodia, a group of female missionaries were leading praise and doing body worship on stage. Tina and I were especially moved by one female missionary's body worship. Her name was Yoosun Kim. After the service was done, we went to her to introduce ourselves and to tell her how we were so moved by her praise and worship. I later participated in prayer meetings held by Ewha Missions (currently called VESSA), which was started by the alumni of Ewha Women's University in Korea. This also led me to get connected to the director of Ewha Missions, Pastor Gil-hyun Kim.

Let me introduce a few female missionaries in Cambodia (order is by whoever came to Cambodia first):

1) Missionary In-soon Kim came to Cambodia in May 1996. She works at the Pailin, where the Khmer Rouge of the northwest corner fought for the last time.

2) Missionary Jeong-young Kim, in August 1996, started ministries in orphanages and kindergartens in Takmao, south of Phnom Penh. At that time, Ms. Kim assigned Pastor Gram Chipp, a senior pastor of ICF Missionary Church, as chairman and started her ministry. In 2017, she began the construction of an elementary, middle and high school. The construction is still in progress.

3) Missionary Yeon-mi Cha, a missionary of YWAM Korea, arrived to Cambodia in November 1996. She first started her ministry at the border of Thailand and is currently doing academic ministry for middle and high school students in Kandal, a suburb of Phnom Penh.

4) Missionary Hye-ryun Kim was a member of GMS (Presbyterian Church in Korea, Hap Dong). She started the Damko church in January 1999 in Damko village of Phnom Penh. She did academic ministry there as well.

5) Missionary Soon-young Jeong, a member of GMS, arrived in April 1999. She founded Hosanna Elementary School in Minchei, which was located near a dumpster. She focused solely on education of the poor. After marrying in 2012, she moved to Pochentong near the airport. Then, she and missionary Hang-cheol Kim combined two middle schools and high schools. She became the principal of the unified school and named it Hosanna School. The school consisted of preschool through high school.

6) Missionary Ok Yoon arrived in October 1999 as a member of Korea Food for Hungry International (KFHI). She ran a preschool and after-school study program. She was a member of the ICF church that we attended.

7) In January 2001, Chul-hee Lee, the first missionary sent to Cambodia through Ewha Missions, started the study room ministry for children in Phnom Penh. As a former nurse, Lee started a health center near Kampong Speu Ewha Srang School, which she runs until today. Lee graduated from Phnom Penh University as a Cambodian Literature major, so she is very fluent in Cambodian.

8) Missionary Gye-gwang Lee arrived in December 2001. She worked for a long time at the Phnom Penh Technical School established by Youngnak Church, Korea. After getting married in 2005, she did industrial park work and church planting. Before her marriage, she worked outstandingly as the vice president of the Korean Missionary Association in Cambodia.

9) Missionary Namsuk Yoo arrived in December 2003 as a joint member of GMP and established a church in Kandal Province. Recently, she established an elementary school and manages it. She married Pastor Kyungho Choi in 2015.

10) Missionary Yoosun Kim arrived in September 2004. She is serving as a principal of the Ewha-surun preschool, elementary school, and middle school established by Ewha Missions (now VESSA). She started

a music school in her early season of missions and trained local piano accompanists. She speaks fluent Cambodian.

11) Missionary Jung-mi Yoo was sent off in November 2004 through Doon Jeon Church in the city of Sung Nam. She started a preschool right next to where I lived. She loved children. We became good friends very quickly. After a while, Yoo went down to Takeo, where there was no preschool available, and established a preschool with tuition. She is still successfully managing the school. She also trained and raised local preschool teachers and sent them to start a study room for elementary school kids from the countryside.

12) Missionary Nam-joo Lee, a music missionary who arrived in May 2005, worked as a piano accompanist for a ICF Church. In 2017, she got into a theological seminary in Singapore and is getting a master's degree.

13) Missionary Dongnam Kang got to Cambodia in May 2005. However, because there are many missionaries in Phnom Penh, she came to the middle east of Cambodia, the border area of northern Thailand, to plant a church. There, she lives with high school girls and trains and raises them as disciples. A local philanthropist donated a large piece of land and Kang's team has been building a school there. The philanthropist is a senior public worker of his hometown Preah Vihear. He became a genuine Christian through missionary Chan-sik Moon. We also dug a well inside the new school. Missionary Kang always stayed at our home whenever she came to Phnom Penh.

14) Missionary Esther Cho arrived in 2006 as a missionary sent by New Life Mission Church (Pastor Young-bae Park) located in Fullerton, California. Prior to coming to Cambodia, she worked as a nurse for 3 years at a mission hospital in Kalimantan, Indonesia. As soon as she came to Cambodia, she went to the Kampot countryside and started a study room for the middle school and high school students. Later in 2017, New Life Mission Church, who had sent Esther, decided to

greatly expand the ministry by building an elementary school, middle school and high school. The construction of the school is currently in progress. Esther was a model missionary who was very adept at speaking Cambodian and living among the local people. Because she previously suffered from incurable malaria without proper treatment while in Indonesia, her body became very weak. Our dental team and missionary David Koo visited her twice to do treatments.

15) Missionary Si-eun Lee arrived in November 2016 through DMS (Presbyterian Church of Korea Daeshin). She does discipleship and children's ministry at Hebron mission hospital.

The above 15 female Korean missionaries are faithful ministers who worked with us directly or indirectly in Cambodia. Our portable dental care team went out to help their ministry whenever they requested.

Missionary John & Debby Coat in Prey Veng

At the request of John and Debby Coat, Baptist missionaries of Prey Veng Province in southeast Cambodia, our team visited there 3 times for portable dental clinics. Their ministry was something we wanted to emulate.

They built a house and lived

Full-denture patient with Debby Coat

with the farmers close to Vietnam in southeast Prey Veng Province near farmland. Most missionaries were reluctant to go into remote areas of the farmland, but their sacrificial lifestyle really challenged us. They lived barefoot following the lifestyle of the farmers. Whenever we went for portable dental missions, Debby, a former nurse practitioner would go around the town to set up appointments for treatment. She also received about 10 cents deposit fee from the people who desired to get treated and gave them the accountability to come on time. With her

The female church member smiling a million-dollar smile with her denture on

help, the ministry was very organized and systematic. Almost no one missed the treatment because of the deposit that was paid. It was good training for John and Debby and an effective ministry for our team as well. John and Debby also built a health center of government in the village. Missionary William Hur, the dental technician, made dentures for one of the female church members from the village. I still remember how overjoyed she was to receive the dentures. She couldn't stop smiling so brightly. Debby called it "a million-dollar smile."

The Ministry of Diamond Canyon Christian Church

Jim Price, the senior pastor of Diamond Canyon Christian Church, California, came to Battambang for missions with his church members. He shared in his testimony about a young mother with a baby from Battambang. This mother didn't have two of her front teeth and had been covering her mouth with her hands all her life. When she received

Diamond Canyon Christian Church mission team from Diamond Bar, California

88

a denture from the mission team, she was overjoyed to have new teeth.

Diamond Canyon Christian Church mission team built a seminary in Battambang, the western border of Thailand, and successfully planted a church there. Pastor Price still visits Battambang every year to give lectures at the seminary. We also went there 3 times to do portable dental clinic with Diamond Canyon Christian Church.

Pastor Jim Price (Diamond Canyon Christian Church)

At that time, the churches transported the members of the village with trucks. They did 2 times for Assembly of God missionary Kelly Ravinates. He runs an elementary school and middle school.

Kreg Mallow Ministry of Ratana Kiri

Kreg Mallow was doing church-planting ministry at Ratana Kiri, a northeastern region located by the Vietnamese border. Missionary Mallow is an OMF missionary, a dentist, and a pastor. We also visited his ministry site 3 times for dental clinics. He helped me a lot in my ministry, as well. He accompanied me whenever he could to go on portable dental missions even when it was outside of his ministry location. Mallow considered portable dental missions to be a very important

ministry, so he genuinely enjoyed going with me. He and his Cambodian wife, Jenny, whom we met in the United States, worked together effectively. One day, we met Jackie Jody, a Bible translator from Switzerland. She lived deep in the mountains, where we were

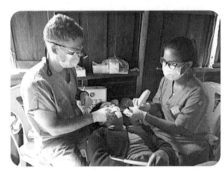

Kreg Mallow (Left)

Dr. Leslie Malone happy holding her twins.

allowed to witness the glorious ministry of translating into Jerai tribe language with the local staff. Through that meeting, missionary Jackie began coming to Phnom Penh for more than 10 years to receive dental treatments.

Furthermore, we cannot forget Dr. Leslie Malone. Dr. Leslie Malone came to Cambodia on the recommendation of Dr. Sam Metcalf, the president of CRM. Dr. Leslie Malone had just graduated from dental school and volunteered to do her internship in the dental clinic of Mercy Medical Center in Cambodia. Dr. Leslie Malone's father is a strong financial supporter and friend of the CRM president. Dr. Leslie Malone was very outgoing and had a great ability to make many friends. The local female Cambodian workers adored Dr. Leslie Malone. She did her best in everything that she did—not only with the portable dental clinic, but with the ministry to the poor and underprivileged as well as the for-profit dental clinic. She worked for a year and a half and did her very best. Dr. Leslie Malone recently got married and gave birth to twins.

Missionary Kisoo Hwang in Tabe

Elder Kisoo Hwang (Gosin Church of Philadelphia; his wife's name is Shinja Kwon) was working as a missionary in a town called Tabe in Kandal Province south of Phnom Penh. Missionary Hwang was from WEC (evangelical mission agency). He faithfully planted churches in Tabe area. My wife and I visited his church several times to worship together. He loved the dental ministry so much that he often asked our team to come. Since Tabe was very close to where we were, we went to do portable dental missions in Tabe more than 10 times. The members of Tabe church and their neighbors were so thankful to receive dental treatments from our missions team. For more complicated treatments, Elder Hwang would bring his church members to our ADC dental clinic in Phnom Penh.

Later in chapter 13 "My Beloved Coworkers", I will share more about missionary Kisoo Hwang.

The Ministry of Missionary Daniel Shinjong Baeq in Kampong Cham

Missionary Shinjong Baeq came to Cambodia early. After studying the language of Khmer, instead of doing ministry at a popular city, he went to Kampong Cham, which is in the countryside. There he actively planted churches. He was a young man, so he would put study materials into his computer to continually study the Khmer language. I was very impressed with missionary Baeq's skill and good character. Since he was so outstanding in every way among Korean missionaries in Cambodia, I personally had high hopes for him. He valued dental ministry so highly and invited short-term mission teams from the United States three times: first to his main church, second to a rural village further than Kampong Cham, and lastly to an island in the middle of the Mekong River. The ministry we did in the latter two was used as a bridge to plant new churches in those areas. Missionary Baeq also built a preschool, which was managed by missionary Hyeja Ha from the United States. He also built a huge orphanage where he brought the children to our dentistry in Phnom Penh.

Missionary Baeq with Cambodian children.

His father-in-law, Dr. Samuel Sungsam Kang, who was the dean of the School of World Missions at Chong-Shin University, recommended missionary Baeq to spend the sabbatical year at Oversea Ministries

Missionary Shin Jong Baeq and his portable dental clinic team going to the island where he served.

Study Center (OMSC). The 10 months stay at OMSC in New Haven CT, was a God-given time of reflection and recovery for the Baeq family. During Missionary Daniel Shinjong Baeq's stay at OMSC, God gave him the opportunity to study at Trinity Evangelical Divinity School in Deerfield, Illinois, which offered him two years of scholarship. Even while he began his studies at Trinity, in his mind there was no doubt about returning to Cambodia. Thus he kept paying rent for the next three years and had fellow missionaries either stay at his house or use it as needed. God, however, made it clear that He had other plans for Missionary Baeq. As he continued to study at Trinity and serve as a home-based missionary, in 2014, Rev. Wonsang Lee, the president of SEED International, recommended Missionary Baeq for the senior pastor's position for Bethel Korean Presbyterian Church(BKPC) in MD. And God, in His sovereignty, placed him at BKPC as the Senior Pastor in August of 2015. His goal is to send out many more missionaries in his place, to awaken and engage churches to missions, to raise up more prayer warriors for world mission, and to someday, God willing, to return to a mission field, himself.

Ministry in Nearby Vicinities and Ministry in Remote Areas

In addition to the ministries I shared earlier, we visited remote areas in the mountainside, prisons, and orphanages. Until Tina and I returned to the United States for good, we completed 71 portable dental clinic missions over 10 years. When mission teams from America came we would take them to a far place (Prey Veng, Battambang, Mondulkiri,

Siem Pang, Koh Kong, etc.) to do portable dental clinics. For places near our clinic, my wife and I, and the local staff team would close the clinic and go on missions for 3 days. For 14 years, the number of dental patients who were cared for by our team were approximately 26,052, as well as 12,350 medical patients. Portable dental missions were very beneficial to Cambodians, especially those who were not able to receive any dental care without them. While valuable, it wasn't necessarily easy.

First, at least one person from our team had to travel to the mission location prior to check the lodging, availability of electricity and place for treatment.

Second, we always had to rent a charter bus and take various equipment. It always took at least 10 hours to get to our destination.

Third, treatment was only done effectively when all the dental equipment was laid out in proper position in advance from Monday to Friday.

Fourth, any complicated treatments could not be done (due to lack of equipment or time limitations). To provide even the basic care of these portable dental clinics took about one-third of our budget. The portable dental ministry required a lot of staff, equipment, and was very expensive.

Although there were many obstacles and limitations in portable dental ministry, we were able to overcome everything with Christ's love and serve wholeheartedly. Portable dental missions was truly a valuable ministry. Through portable dental ministry, we also saved permanent teeth for many of the young children and teenagers we treated. I'm mentioning this because permanent teeth are very important.

Our dental team walking across the bridge to get to Koh Kong region

"Recalling the Ministry of Portable Medical/dental Care"

I'd like to add one more story about one of the patients who was in her early 40s and in the terminal stage of oral cancer. When we saw her, there was nothing we could do. So our team started prayer and shared the gospel with her. She accepted the Lord Jesus Christ as her savior. Two weeks later she passed away. She lived in Neak Leung, Prey Veng Province.

At that time OMF missionary Hak-yeon Cho informed Dr. Donald Lee, MD, that she had passed away. Dr. Lee, along with his colleagues pharmacist David Lee, and Steven Kim, DDS, together donated $3,000 for her funeral service and to help with living expenses for her remaining family. (The cancer patient is pictured on p.103, #5)

I would like to share some thoughts as I look back on the memories of our 71 portable dental missions. Our team was always ready to leave home whenever we were called, even when we had to go to a remote place. We would sleep at farmhouses without complaining. We thought we were specially blessed when there was a guest house. However, it was always unlikely that these remote places would have proper lodging for our team. Usually farmhouses in the countryside are 2-story houses built out of wood. The rooftops of the houses of the poor are covered with palm leaves. People with a little more money would use tiles. Livestock slept on the first floor and people on the second floor. Houses in the countryside would easily flood when it rained a lot.

For that reason, the columns of the first floor are very tall and the stairs are very narrow and steep. Our team was usually separated into 3-4 houses and it was a requirement for our team to bring portable mattresses and mosquito nets. If you slept without a mosquito net, you would get bitten all over by mosquitoes.

But, in fact, what was scarier than mosquitoes was the toilet. There was no toilet inside the house. Their backyard is the restroom.If you wanted to go to the bathroom at night, you would have to turn on the flashlight, carefully walk down the narrow and steep stairs and squat in the backyard under the stars of the night sky, listening to the sounds of the insects. It was somewhat romantic, while at the same time embarrassing. Since going to the bathroom was so difficult, I would just choose to sleep all night instead of waking up in the middle of the night to go to the bathroom. The kitchen was located upstairs at the corner of the

bamboo-made living room. Chopped wood was used to start fires for cooking. It was very rare for houses to have electricity. Lights used at night were very dim since they were connected to a battery. It was impossible to read books under that light,

Chopped wood for the kitchen to be used for cooking

so when the sun went down, there was not much you could do, so you would just go to bed early in the evening. Lying inside a mosquito net with a bunch of buzzing mosquitoes,

Usually I would begin to pray for my supporters all around the world. I would fall asleep pretty quickly when I tried to remember every supporter's name and face. However, when I still couldn't fall asleep, I would count to 100. My last prayer was usually to fall into a deep sleep where I wouldn't wake up at all until morning.

Places with lodging for guests are usually big villages. Even with lodging, our team couldn't sleep well since the dogs in town would bark all night. A group of dogs would make an eerie crying sound together, which distracted us from sleeping. Cambodians love dogs. Dogs are everywhere. If you were to go out for a walk, you had to carry a stick because dogs were rarely on a leash.

It was October 1, 2018, in the last year of our ministry when I left our lodging to take a walk. Three or four dogs were playing on the street and suddenly one dog jumped at me and bit my left knee. I started bleeding. It was Sunday that day, so the Pasteur lab was closed. I couldn't receive vaccines to prevent rabies. I called the emergency room of a nearby hospital, and there was still no vaccine there. I had to wait until Monday to get a vaccination at the Pasteur lab. I received the injection once every week for 3 consecutive weeks. I observed the dog that bit me and thankfully it showed no symptoms of rabies.

When Tina and I arrived in Cambodia in 2004, one of the four vaccinations we were required to get was the rabies vaccination. However, 14 years had passed since we got the vaccination, so I was supposed to get the vaccination again. I personally have a fear about rabies, so I was very stressed when I was bitten by that dog. The reason for the fear was

my experience in the army in South Korea. A soldier with rabies came to Mobile Army Surgical Hospital and there was nothing we could do. We had sent the patient to evacuate hospital in Wonju where there was nothing that could be done, but just wait for the patient to die. It was 50 years ago, right after the Korean War ended, rabies spread in my hometown, Goheung-eup, Jeollanam-do. I can still vividly remember how the police were shooting and killing all the dogs they saw.

Generators are a must for portable dental ministry. You don't need electricity to remove teeth, but in order to do fillings, the electricity is mandatory. You have to bring at least one 5KW generator, but sometimes this even breaks down. Whenever a

Mr. Seing, the bus driver, fixing the generator

breakdown happened, Mr. Seing, the bus driver, would fix the carburetor, and we would pray on the side with anxiety.

It took some time to bring in a technician, but the bigger problem was that we had to stop all our ministry until the generator was fixed. On one occasion, a local pastor told me to come without a generator because they had one, so I went without it. However, it was a generator made in China that looked large but had a very low power output that could not power our unit. After that, we would always carry our 5KW generator to portable dental missions. We would use our own generator to the fullest and sell it after a year then buy a new one again. For large ministries, we would take two generators.

Looking back at those memories, it was definitely difficult, but everything was covered by God's grace.

Traditional Weddings

In all the time I was in Cambodia, I never saw any "modern", or western-style, weddings. Weddings were still very much in the traditional style. April was the busiest month for weddings in Cambodia. It is after the rice harvest is done and before the raining season comes in May. April is considered to be off-season for farmers and the best month for weddings. Cambodian New Year is in April, so everyone stops working and goes back to their hometown. This is the hottest season, too.

Typically, weddings in Cambodia are held for three days. On the first day, the groom goes to the bride's house with a dowry and gives it to the in-laws. According to the standard of 2017, the dowry should be at least $2000. If the amount is larger, the groom is usually showing off his wealth, and if it is less than the standard, the bride's side would think that they were being looked down on by the groom's family. It is very common for Cambodian men not to be able to afford the dowry, so they remain as old bachelors. When the official meeting between the two families is done, a Buddhist monk or a Christian pastor if the couple is Christian, would come and bless the couple.

On the second day, both sides of the family and their close relatives place various fruits on a tray and follow the groom. They line up with wedding gifts and enter the bride's house. After everyone is seated, a Buddhist monk gives a prayer of blessing. In the Christian ceremony, the bride and the groom wash each other's feet. Around 5pm, a reception is held for all the invited guests. The guest gives a gift of money as congratulations, and enters the reception. At the end of the dinner, the bride and the groom change into a wedding outfit. They change their outfits at least 5 times. Then the entertainment begins.

On the third day, the families and the close relatives gather to tie the bride and groom's wrists with red threads. In many cases, this part of the ceremony is omitted. At the mission dental clinic where I worked, the ceremony was a mixture of Christianity and Buddhism. It was the wedding of a chief doctor. The bride wasn't a believer and her family was conservative Buddhist. The mother of the chief doctor was a devout Christian, so the wedding ended up as both Christian and Buddhist. A Christian pastor would pray and officiate the wedding and a Buddhist monk would come out to chant the Buddhist scripture. Of course, this mixed wedding ceremony was done upon agreement of both sides of the family. Generally, weddings are held in one style of religion.

Teaching at IU Dental School

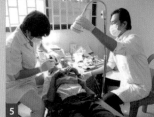

PHOTO CAPTIONS
1. *Team waiting for the bus*
2. *Triaz with a patient*
3. *Volunteer hygienist from the US*
4. *Dr. Tom Love extracting*
5. *Senior dental students*
6. *Treatment floor*
7. *Dr. Buntha and Seila*

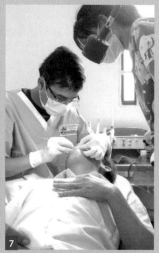

100

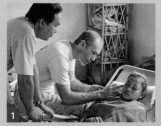

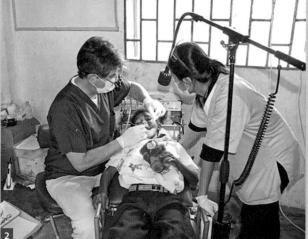

PHOTO CAPTIONS
1. Medical doctor from MTI with student
2. Dr. Chiang Ly
3. Dentist and spouse from MTI
4. Devotion time
5. Sharing the gospel and praying
6. Team photo

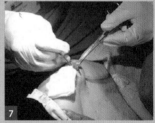

PHOTO CAPTIONS
1. Deacon Kim from Inland Presby. Church
2. Inland Church team (Pomona, CA)
3. Steven Kim, DDS & Elder Sang Paik, DDS
4. Pedodontist from MTI
5. Rev. Dae Sung Kang & his wife
6. My sister Myung & pastor's wife cutting hair
7. Donald Lee, MD removes benign tumor
8. Pharmacist David Lee giving out medicine

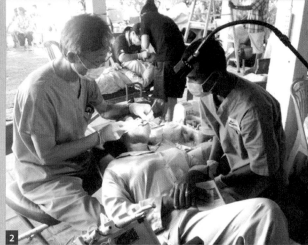

PHOTO CAPTIONS
1. Donald Lee, MD examining a patient
2. Assistant Chan with Dr. Cho
3. Teaching students at small room
4. Looks like 3 sets of lower front teeth
5. Terminal oral cancer patient
6. Inland church team photo
7. Treating Buddhist monk at Preah Vihear
8. 5 people baptized by Pastor Timothy Ith at Kondal

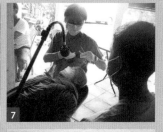

"

And now, compelled by the Spirit, I am going to Jerusalem, not knowing what will happen to me there. I only know that in every city the Holy Spirit warns me that prison and hardships are facing me. However, I consider my life worth nothing to me; my only aim is to finish the race and complete the task the Lord Jesus has given me—the task of testifying to the good news of God's grace (Acts 20:22-24, NIV).

8

Church-Planting Ministry

Tina and I, along with a local pastor, did church-planting ministry for one and a half years (latter half of 2005 to the end of 2007)

Building 190 Cottages and Church Inaugural Service

Evangelist Hang Abraham Simting always had a heart for the poor. He was the fiancé (now husband) of our clinic's employee Sophen and was a pastor studying in seminary with the scholarship we provided. He used to evangelize to the people of Andong village, the worst slum in Cambodia. This was a village far west of downtown Phnom Penh, where the poor who lived next to the royal palace were forcibly moved to. The government relocated more than 5,000 people to Andong, distributing 4m x 6m of land per family. The toilet was shared by all the villagers.

The drinking water was shared from a water tank installed by UNICEF. In Andong village, no jobs were available. No transportation was available since it was far from the city.

For these reasons, life in Andong became more and more difficult over time. Pastor

Missionary Hur and myself (right) building a thatched house. Simting is on the roof.

Simting just started doing Bible studies in an existing thatched cottage and shared the gospel.

In seeing the harsh environment of Andong village, our poverty-relief missions effort (InnerCHANGE) first built 40 cottages for the residents with young children, who were living

Assistance Pastor Abraham of Teumoda Church giving a benediction.

in thin tarpaulin tents. Babpur Missions of Dail Community of Korea built 40 houses and Seattle Presbyterian Church sent emergency relief money to build 110 houses. On November 12, 2006, the inaugural service of Teumoda Church was held at a warehouse rented by missionary Jeong-gyu Choi of Babpur Missions, Korea. Assistant Pastor Hang Abraham Simting started Teumoda (which means Rock) Church. I was officially inaugurated as an elder and also became a treasurer. After only about 6 months, the Teumoda church grew and became very tight and uncomfortable, so we built a wooden building across from the Babpur Mission. Mark, the team leader of InnerCHANGE often came and preached and Tina and Leng Chan Heng served in the Sunday School. As we were staying in Andong we would go out for portable dental clinic. For dentures and complicated treatments, we brought the villagers to our dental clinic CSI. One time we brought a patient to our clinic and made full dentures for him. However, after a month, he came to Sunday service without the upper denture. When I asked him what happened, he said he lost it when he was drunk. I asked the pastor if we should make another denture for the church member, but the pastor said no since the church member would lose it again. It's still sad when I think about the man who lost the denture.

Still, 10 years have passed, and I still can't forget the blessings and grace I experienced at Andong village.

Well-Digging Ministry

Cambodia's water condition is horrible. Regular tap water can never be used as drinking water. People in the city use purifiers. On the contrary, people in countryside collect rainwater for drinking. Tina and I also launched a well-digging ministry. We dug wells in 3 different locations, and the villagers were able to drink clean water from them.

1. Well of Kampong Speu Province

This came about when we visited the house of our helper Sreymom in Kampong Speu Province. Her family would walk to fetch water from a well far from their home, so we dug a well in her house. We also made a flush toilet. It was so good to see her family drinking clean water and enjoying living in a clean environment.

2. Mondulkiri Well

The village of Mondulkiri was located by the mountains, so water was scarce during the dry season. Since it was in the mountains, digging the ground couldn't raise groundwater. We had to spend 5 times more than the regular cost to dig wells at 2 locations in the village. But still, with the new wells, we were able to provide clean water to the villagers.

Traditional costume in Bousra, Mondulkiri

3. Preah Vihear's Well

Dongnam Kang, was working as a missionary in Preah Vihear. We spent $2,600 to dig a well inside the school founded by missionary Kang. I received the total donation needed for digging wells from Orange Hill Presbyterian Church, my home church in the United States.

Scholarship Payment Ministry

We had provided scholarships for 7 years to two National Dental College students: Buntha and Sambo. Buntha and Sambo went to school every day while eating, sleeping, and working at our dental clinic.

Dr. Donald Lee performing treatment during missions

Scholarships were also given to five other students. I helped one student from National Medical School for 2 years. He was recommended by an OMF missionary Yewon Choo, one from IU medical school for 4 years, and another from IU Dental School, and another from University of Puthisastra Dental School for 4 years. In fact, this scholarship program was a valuable ministry led by deacon Donald Lee, MD (Inland Korean Church). Dr. Lee came to Cambodia 4 times as a leader of short-term missions teams from Inland Church. Through those missions, he treated many patients in Cambodia.

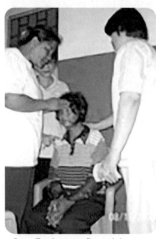

Bong Tom's evangelism ministry

Bong Tom's Evangelism Ministry

Bong Tom was a single lady in her late 30s working as a janitor at the dental clinic. After receiving Jesus, she led so many people to Christ. Evangelism was her special gift given from God. She would proudly tell people that she married Jesus. She also used her experience of growing up in poverty to reach out to the poor. Her words presenting the gospel message to people moved many people's hearts. Bong Tom was so gifted that she was invited to an Evangelism Conference as a guest speaker to share her testimony.

My Wife Tina's Beautiful Partnership and Dedication

I would like to share particularly the great devotion of my
wife, Tina (Youngja in Korean),
shown to the Cambodian church.
Above all, she was a prayer war-
rior. Whatever happened, she
would quietly pray to God and
receive answers or solutions from Him.

Although we are so fragile like a broken vessel, God still uses us

Her naturally bright and cheerful temperament given from God was used greatly in training, encouraging and comforting the local staff. She trained Lachana, the receptionist at our clinic, and encouraged her to later serve as the manager. Her gift and dedication also stood out whenever she was leading the staff team in worship. The portable dental clinic was able to run so smoothly due to my wife Tina's faithful work in the background. She took care of the short-term team from the US as well as provided food for our employees. On top of this, Tina welcomed the locals with great care. Tina encouraged the employees to give thanks to God whenever they worked saying, "We will eventually leave Cambodia but you will remain here and continue to proclaim the gospel of Jesus. Therefore, we cannot do this ministry without your in-volvement and help." She continually impressed this on the employees to do their best, as she always did her best.

Tina's partnership and commitment was like the one that deacon Priscilla and Phoebe had shown to the Apostle Paul. We had helped ignite the fire of the gospel by building churches, digging wells, provid-ing scholarships to young students who couldn't afford schooling, and training our disciples at home while working hard together at the clinic.

"

Consider it pure joy, my brothers and sisters, whenever you face trials of many kinds, because you know that the testing of your faith produces perseverance. Let perseverance finish its work so that you may be mature and complete, not lacking anything. If any of you lacks wisdom, you should ask God, who gives generously to all without finding fault, and it will be given to you. But when you ask, you must believe and not doubt, because the one who doubts is like a wave of the sea, blown and tossed by the wind. That person should not expect to receive anything from the Lord. Such a person is double-minded and unstable in all they do (James 1:2-8, NIV).

9

Teaching at a Dental School

Private University (International University)

Meeting missionary Callum Durward (pedodontist and founder of the dental college) gave me the opportunity to fulfill my dream as a missionary. During the beginning of the civil war in Cambodia, missionary Durward worked at a refugee camp in Thailand on the border of Cambodia to treat the refugees. He was a missionary sent from One-2-One Missions in New Zealand. After the 1993 Paris Peace Agreement, he moved to Phnom Penh and established an orphanage and a poverty-relief ministry. He also started a prison ministry. The poverty-relief and prison ministries are still very active. Then, in 2006, Callum Durward was asked to build a dental school at International University (IU). After he established the dental school, he worked as the dean for a long time.

One day in 2007, before the fall se-

Dr. Callum Durward as dean of IU School of Dentistry

mester began, Dr. Durward visited me. He had heard about me through Dr. Serey, the president of Cambodia Christian Dental Association. He asked me to teach at IU School of Dentistry. In that moment, my heart was filled with such gratitude and joy. I thought in my head, "Oh, God had already planned everything and led me here!"

How eager I was to teach at the dental school in Cambodia! The dream I had of sharing advanced techniques and skills learned in the United States with Cambodian students was finally coming true. I immediately welcomed and accepted the request.

First, I started with one subject: root canal therapy (endodontics). My first class consisted of only 15 students, but it was a fun, rewarding and a blessed time. Cambodia was very behind in regards to root canal therapy.

During my 1-year sabbatical (January-December 2008) in the United States, I diligently prepared study materials for the dental school in Cambodia. I visited my alma mater, USC, and obtained the endodontics training manual from the professor of endodontics. On the following Sabbath, I met Dr. Yaara Berdan, the head professor of endodontics at the USC Undergraduate School. At that time I explained to her about the poor condition of endodontics education in Cambodia and asked for her help. She looked highly upon my ministry and was more than willing to help in any way. She also handed me a business card to contact her whenever I needed her help. I visited her at USC in April 2019 and asked for updated materials for endodontics courses. I was planning to teach during a 3-month dental mission to the National Dental University in Ethiopia. Dr. Berdan took 2 hours to photocopy all the materials and handed them to me. She was such a wonderful person and doctor.

Myungsung Hospital Dental Ministry in Ethiopia

Myungsung Hospital in the capital city Addis Ababa is considered the best hospital in Ethiopia. It has a prestigious medical school within the hospital compound. I was asked to train 5 Ethiopian dentists by missionary Tak Jum Jeong. He is a highly skilled lab technician with strong faith. He runs a dental department because the dentist missionary left 3 years ago and no replacement was found. I was also asked to teach at National Dental School through a part-time oral surgeon professor working in Myungsung who introduced me to the dean.

The dental department is equipped with expensive chairs, CT scan and dental materials from Korea. The hospital was founded by the large Myungsung church in Seoul, Korea. Reverend Sam Whan Kim (former senior pastor of the church) was on a mission trip to Africa, where he visited several countries where church missionaries work. He visited Ethiopia who participated in the Korean War to find out any mission opportunities.

Reverend Kim met the prime minister of Ethiopia, who said we need a good hospital desperately. As a result Myungsung hospital was established in 2004.

The dental education in Ethiopia is poor. Many private dental schools do not have proper equipment and severely lack dental materials. Even at the top National Dental School in Addis Ababa, half of the beautiful dental chairs donated by Sweden are not working because of no dental technicians and no spare parts. The light is out but there are no light bulbs. The water spray doesn't work because there are no spare plastic tubes.

I taught endodontics and basic restorative therapy at both Myungsung dental department and taught senior students for 3 months. Tina helped with organizing books at the medical school library.

I informed Sweden's aid agency what is happening with the good-willed chairs and endodontics equipment. I got a letter informing me they sent the people, checked it out, and got a report from Sweden. I hope students may use the repaired equipment by now.

Interaction with Students

After my first sabbatical year, in January 2009 I returned to Cambodia to teach at IU Dental School. At that time, the quality of the periodontal course (gum treatment) was so bad that I had to teach this course along with the nerve treatment course. Because evangelism was not permitted at school, I invited my students to my home and taught them the Bible. Except for one female student, all 14 students, came to my home to do the first Bible study. Most likely all of them came out of courtesy. However, 5-6 students consistently came after that, so I was able to teach the Bible continuously.

Endodontics Specialist Course

As time passed, Dr. Durward, struggled with the lack of resources and poor level of the endodontics (root canal therapy) class. After his relentless persuasion, he was able to bring over 3 head professors of endodontics: two professors from Australia (Steven Cohn, Paul Abbott) and one from New Zealand (Peter Cathro). Dr. Cathro was in charge of an endodontics specialist course at IU. He also invited two other professors.They did not hesitate to fly for 7 hours from the southern hemisphere to come to Cambodia once a month. They brought endodontics materials and the necessary tools for teaching.

When the professor team was ready, it was time for me to recruit the students. Our goal was to recruit 7 students, but there were no applicants. As a last resort, Dr. Durward and I persuaded some of the alumni. The students for the endodontics class consisted of 5 people: 3

Class with Professor Steven Cohn (second from the right)

of my students, a doctor and an alumnus of National University, and me. I applied because although I was a professor, I was not a specialist. At that time, endodontics was not popular in Cambodia because dentists

Professors (second from the left, professors Yan Markus and Steven Cohn and dean Som Vichet) and four students who completed the 3-year endodontics specialist course.

couldn't make much money out of root canal treatment. Many unlicensed dentists would do the root canal treatment at a very low cost. The doctor from the National University quit after a month, perhaps because the class was harder than he expected. Four students including myself remained. Finally, the endodontics Specialist course was delivered at IU School of Dentistry. I was proud of myself for starting something that I'd never even thought of. I started at the age of 72 and ended at 75. It was definitely impossible for me to complete the course without God's amazing grace.

The professors from Australia moved all their expensive instruments and treatment materials personally and taught the students wholeheartedly. We were very moved by their hard work and devotion and definitely enjoyed the benefits from their commitment. Three years later (2017), 4 endodontists were produced in Cambodia. It was not easy for me to study at an old age and complete the course. However, God gave me strength to go through the difficult process and overcome each obstacle.

I personally learned so much through the 3-year course. I learned to treat the original teeth and preserve them instead of extracting. I was able to apply that to our patients. And in carrying on this deposit of endodontics education, I went to Ethiopia from June to August 2019 and taught endodontics at a college (see chapter 14).

At IU, as I was teaching the students, I was able to see that dental schools in Cambodia were also very behind in periodontics (gum treatment) and dentures. For that reason, I focused on endodontics, periodontics, and dentures and did my best to teach the students. I took care of the upper-division students who completed the lower-division courses. I diligently taught all the things that the dentists should know. I also created opportunities for the students to do their field work and clinical training at my clinic. After my retirement from missions in December 2017, I went back to Cambodia in 2018 to teach students for the last time. This visit in 2018 was for the purpose of re-teaching

my course on amalgam fillings to the upcoming class of students. It needed to be repeated because more than half of the class had been caught cheating on the final examination. So, the students were required to take the 5-week course again.

Students from International University

When I left back to the US after the semester was done in 2018, the 6th graders and alumni threw a grand farewell party for me. Also, the dean and professors planned a farewell party for me. Those were unforgettable moments and a great privilege God had provided.

To tell you the truth, there were times that I was pressured by the school to be easy with grading. I was asked not to fail many students, but to pass them. However, it was very difficult for me to do that and I didn't let anyone under 60 points pass the class. One time, about two-thirds of the class couldn't pass and all of them had to retake the final exam. Repeating the exam and the whole process was very hard, but rewarding. Through facing that adversity, I believe the students were trained to be dentists with proper knowledge and virtue.

Introduction of the National Examination System

In the past, Cambodia had serious issues with corruption in the dental school system. Some students were admitted because of their academic skill, but others came through bribes. As a result, there was a large gap between the students in terms of academic level. It was very difficult to send those students with no academic rigor to the upper divisions.

Many years later, a son of an influential minister returned to Cambodia after graduating from a Ph.D program at UCLA Medical School, and became the president of the National College of Public Health. All medical-related schools (medicine, dentistry, pharmacy, nursing, etc.) were under the National College of Public Health. As soon as he took the position, he ordered all medical and dental school students to take a state exam to obtain the official license. Until then, there were no state exams and students could simply graduate from school and get a license. Finally, there was a nationally enforced exam for medical and dental schools. Though it was actually illegal, the president photocopied the exams from the United States and gave them to the professors to use as a reference for creating the state exams. Students from the National Dental School were against the idea of a state exam, so they boycotted taking them. However, I continued to teach the students at IU. I was asked to prepare classes for the exam since I had already experienced taking the exams in the States. It had been a long time since I graduated from dental school in the United States, but I willingly accepted the dean's offer and helped the students prepare for the state exam. I, too, studied as much as the students in order to teach them and prepare them for the national exam.

The national examination became a norm and finally led to qualified students studying and taking the exam. The gap between the academic

Professor Frank Cho as a proctor

level of the students narrowed drastically, as well. Even today, 200-300 questions from the US national exam are selected and translated into Cambodian. National exams are not too difficult since they are made from already existing questions. Another change of policy is that all the medical and dental school applicants must take written exams by the Ministry of Health and Welfare (MHW). Newly accepted dental and medical students are assigned to different universities by the MHW. College-prep students are asked to write down the universities they desire to attend. Then, acceptance is determined by their grades. The reason for accepting students by their grades is to prevent illegal admission practices of medical and dental schools, which were so common in Cambodia before. Ever since the Ministry of Health and Welfare took over control, illegal admission practices have been much more difficult, leading to higher-caliber students getting in.

Microbiology Education

Dr. Durward attended a dental conference of the International Association for Dental Research in the Philippines. There, Dr. Durward met Professor Gak-gyun Kim, the head professor of the Department of Microbiology at Seoul National University Dental School. Dr. Durward shared about the weaknesses of the microbiology classes in Cambodia. Thankfully our appeal moved Professor Kim's heart. Dr. Kim came and taught the subject for 2 months during his winter break (2012). I found out later that Dr. Kim's father was a pastor, and he is still teaching microbiology at a university where Durward is the dean of University of

Puthisastra Dental School (UP).

Looking back at my 10 years of teaching at the dental school (Fall 2007-2018), it was truly a time of hard work and devoting myself to the students. Even as I was teaching at the college, I never stopped sharing the gospel with students. Although the fruits weren't too visible, I know God, who led me to plant the seeds of the gospel, will also grow them. Having a confident hope that these seeds of the gospel would one day reap a harvest. I left Cambodia in October 2018. I was able to leave Cambodia by trusting in God's promise that those who sow with tears will reap with songs of joy (Psalms 126:5-6, NIV).

Sending Students to the US to Raise Future Periodontal Professors

Dr. Mana Seth was the daughter of a successful entrepreneur and was able to afford the tuition to attend UCLA. She was also very skillful as a dentist, so I had a dream to see her raised one day as a periodontal professor.

So I shared my dream with Dr. Jone Kim (Osstem implant instructor, commissioned from GDA) who came to Cambodia 3 times as a lecturer, of my hope to raise a Cambodian student to become a periodontal professor in the United States. Dr. Kim was colleagues with a man named Dr. Steven Lee, who was the director of the 2-year program at UCLA (DDS bachelor's degree program) and he offered to introduce us. With the email address I got from Dr. Jone Kim, I emailed Dr. Steven Lee right away. I asked if there

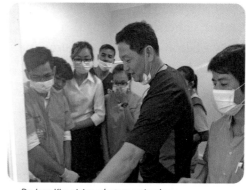

Dr. Jone Kim giving a lecture on implants

119

Dr. Frank Cho and dental students at IU

were any special opportunities for a student from Cambodia at UCLA's 2-year program. I met him at his office. He said the selection committee would consider accepting this Cambodian student if she met certain qualifications. This 2-year program was offered to students with outstanding grades, with the majority of the students accepted coming from India. I immediately suggested Dr. Seth Mana to take the TOEFL and Part I & II exams to apply for UCLA's DDS program. Dr. Seth Mana visited the United States 3 times and passed the Part I & II exams, but has struggled to pass the TOEFL exam. She is currently taking care of her sick father and working as a dentist. I am still waiting for the day that she becomes a periodontal professor to teach Cambodian students. It is both Mana's dream and my hope as well.

"Consider it pure joy, my brothers and sisters, whenever you face trials of many kinds, because you know that the testing of your faith produces perseverance. Let perseverance finish its work so that you may be mature and complete, not lacking anything" (James 1:2-4, NIV).

EXPERIENCING CAMBODIAN CULTURE

Khmer Language

Cambodia's Khmer language has its origins in Sanskrit, which has been passed down from northern India. The language is very complex and has 33 consonants and 35 vowels. It is difficult to write and to pronounce the words. There are four different types of "T" pronunciations. Even the locals who have completed high

school education can have a hard time reading some words. Typing the language on a computer also takes a long time because vowels are written above, below, and to the side of consonants. Khmer people value their characters very much. There is strong opposition from Buddhist monks against any adaptation of the characters. Thailand simplified their alphabet and made it easier for people to type on the computer. However, Cambodia is still sticking with the old forms. As a foreigner, I believe it is an urgent matter for Cambodia to reform their alphabet, which will aid in the modernization of the country. Cambodia's language is also different for each social class. There are words that are used by the monks and the intellectuals. And there are words used by the working class. Even if you study the language well in a school, sometimes you don't understand the conversations of the working class. Since the Bible was translated by the monks, many parts were written in sophisticated language. I hope that text reform will take place in Cambodia as soon as possible so that the Bible can reach the common people.

ក ka [kɒː]	ខ kha [kʰɒː]	គ ko [kɔː]	ឃ kho [kʰɔː]	ង ŋo [ŋɔː]
ច ca [cɒː]	ឆ cha [cʰɒː]	ជ jo [cɔː]	ឈ jho [cʰɔː]	ញ ño [ɲɒː]
ដ ṭa [ɗɒː]	ឋ ṭha [tʰɒː]	ឌ ḍo [ɗɔː]	ឍ ḍho [tʰɔː]	ណ ṇo [nɒː]
ត ta [tɒː]	ថ tha [tʰɒː]	ទ do [tɔː]	ធ dho [tʰɔː]	ន no [nɔː]
ប pa [ɓɒː]	ផ pha [pʰɒː]	ព bo [pɔː]	ភ bho [pʰɔː]	ម mo [mɔː]
ស sa [sɒː]	ហ ha [hɒː]	យ yo [jɔː]	រ ro [rɔː]	ល lo [lɔː]
ឡ la [lɒː]	អ ʔa [ʔɒː]	វ vo [wɔː]		

"

In the presence of God and of Christ Jesus, who will judge the living and the dead, and in view of his appearing and his kingdom, I give you this charge: Preach the word; be prepared in season and out of season; correct, rebuke and encourage—with great patience and careful instruction. For the time will come when people will not put up with sound doctrine. Instead, to suit their own desires, they will gather around them a great number of teachers to say what their itching ears want to hear. They will turn their ears away from the truth and turn aside to myths. But you, keep your head in all situations, endure hardship, do the work of an evangelist, discharge all the duties of your ministry (2 Timothy 4:1-5, NIV).

10

For-Profit
Dental Clinic

Plan to Establish a For-Profit Dental Clinic

At this point, I would like to share how we established a dental clinic as a subsidiary of CRM's Business as Missions (BAM) ministry. So, actually I worked in 2 dental clinics. One was the continuing clinic for the poor that we started in 2005, and the other one was a "for-profit" ministry.

I finished my 1-year sabbatical in 2008 in the United States and returned to Cambodia in January 2009. During my sabbatical, the Cambodian army commandeered our building for military use, and told us we needed to vacate the building immediately. As a result, our dental clinic which was in the Southern Baptist Mission Hospital had to move to Tulkok temporarily. At that time, some of the dental equipment and materials from the clinic were temporarily moved to the new clinic in Tulkok, while the rest was stored in my home because of limited space at the new facility. Later, the equipment was moved to Ratana Plaza and the clinic was reopened. At that time, the 750 dollars we were being charged for rent at Tulkok clinic was too much for us, so I reported to the department of InnerCHANGE of CRM. It is then that they suggested Business as Missions (BAM) or Enterprise International at CRM.

The head director for BAM was Colin Crawwel who suggested that we make a plan to establish a paid, for-profit dental clinic. So I came up with a plan to set up a for-profit (BAM) dental clinic to target the upper class, and would require us to have 2 properly equipped treatment chairs and X-rays. Finally, BAM approved our plan and provided $50,000. I started purchasing dental equipment: the treatment chairs and X-ray machines were purchased locally, but all other equipment had to be purchased from the United States. Buying and bringing the equipment from the US was very difficult. However, the only way to get high-quality equipment was to source it from the US. After the preparations, we were finally able to open the for-profit clinic at Tulkok in Apiril 2009.

Ministry of the Paid Dental Clinic in Tulkok

We were able to make money by opening the for-profit dental clinic in Tulkok. Business as Missions is a tentmaking strategy that was evaluated very positively by the Lausanne Congress. We put this strategy into practice on the actual mission field, and we were able to realize very good results. I can't deny that the ministry profited very much from having a US dental license holder. Still, there were many difficulties in starting a for-profit clinic. Since we couldn't find new dental equipment and materials, we had no choice but to buy them from the US Yes, equipment that was made in the USA was the best and most advanced, so though difficult, we still purchased and brought them over to Cambodia.

The main clientele of the for-profit clinic were Korean missionaries, OMF missionaries, upper-class Cambodian people, and Korean businessmen. Through this dental business, we were able to realize some profit. Eventually, we were able to pay back the $38,000 we received from the headquarters. We only spent $38,000 of the $50,000 we received. We paid everything back within 5 years of opening the clinic.

In the early days of the clinic, we gave a 25% discount to Korean missionaries. However, the calculation became very complicated, so we ended the discount system. Even though our clinic was more expensive than others, people still came to ours to get treated because all the equipment was modern and the staff team was very skilled and knowledgeable. Later on, we were still able to do some treatment for the poor. They were Vietnamese children, seminary students, and other patients brought to us by missionaries because the dental clinic in the mission hospital is located far away.

Dental Clinic of Mercy Medical Center (MMC) by the Tonle Basak River

The temporary dental clinic in Tulkok was relocated to the Tonle Basak River in the southeast. At this clinic, we mostly treated the locals. The patients were asked to cover only about 10% of their payment and the rest was supported with funds given by the missions department. Even when the patients were very poor, we asked them to pay at least a dollar. The intention was to educate them and build self-reliance. The locals were already forming habits of receiving charity and relying on missionaries or outsiders without self-reliance. We tried our best to fix this negative pattern through our payment system, so they could take ownership of overcoming problems on their own.

At that time, I was extremely busy and tired since I was teaching at IU, doing ministry for the poor, and running the for-profit clinic. Sometimes I would also go on the portable dental missions and that made my life even busier. With Dr. Makara treating patients along with me, and with Dr. Buntha assisting me, I was able to take a breath. The for-profit clinic also helped the dental students at IU to do field training. Furthermore, the students were able to come and practice dentistry at the mission dental clinic as well. Implant treatment was a must at the for-profit clinic, so we wanted Dr. Makara to go to the States to take a course on implants. However, receiving a US visa was very complicated. As we were struggling and waiting to receive a visa, Dr. Sam Metcalf, the president of CRM, became Dr. Makara's financial sponsor. After Dr. Makara received the visa, he was able to go to the States, finish the implant course, and return with good grades. Also, we later received

Sam, the president of CRM and Dr. Makara

Dr. Kim (Osstem Implant Lecturer), who was commissioned by GDA (Global Dental Alliance), and visited Cambodia 3 times at his own expense. He came and gave lectures on implant techniques. With the most updated implant techniques and knowledge, we were able to provide quality dental care to patients in Cambodia.

Later, when I finished my ministry in December 2017 and returned to the US, I decided to come back and visit Cambodia. I came in May 2018 and found that many Korean customers stopped coming to the for-profit clinic. All the American patients were still using the clinic, but for some reason only the Korean clientele stopped coming. I've found that Americans tend to develop trust and relationships with the institutions and organizations in the areas they live. However, Koreans tend to feel comfortable around other Koreans, and trust and rely on each other. My return to the US had caused many of the Korean patients to leave the clinic as a result. I felt very bad for Dr. Makara since he didn't quite understand the Korean culture.

Cooperation with the Christian Dental Association of Cambodia

Every month, I attended a meeting held by Christian Dental Association of Cambodia. For 2 years, I gave lectures there on partial, full denture, and endodontics. Under the supervision of missionary Yewon Choo and Chern Chern Choo, I also took charge of supplementary education. While these 3 subjects were taught in the schools, none of the doctors were able to learn them thoroughly, and so we offered them supplementally.

All these lectures took place at the largest church in Cambodia— New Life Fellowship Church. For the first 30 minutes, senior Pastor Taing Vek Huong preached the gospel, and then for the next hour we had lectures. Despite his busy schedule, Pastor Taing was faithful to share the gospel with these dentists because he truly believed that it was of critical importance for them to believe in Jesus. We invited many dentists who were non-believers. My lectures were translated by Dr. Chern Chern Choo. President Dr. Serey was a deacon of this church and his wife was a former student of mine at IU.

The lecture went for about an hour, and the remaining time was used for practice. Dental materials that I brought from the United States helped a lot during the practice time. Through this relationship, we were able to go on portable dental missions organized by the Christian Dental Missions of Cambodia. At that time, Dr. Makara, with the portable dental equipment, led the missions upon the organization's request. Many doctors and nurses also came with us, so the ministry was even more effective than usual. When Dr. Serey, who was a very sincere man, was the president of the Christian Dental Mission for 10 years, we were able to work together very effectively. By the time I was returning home, he was also planning to retire and looking for a successor. He is married to a Christian dentist whom I taught, and has 2 children.

" Now the Lord is the Spirit, and where the
Spirit of the Lord is, there is freedom. And
we all, who with unveiled faces contemplate
the Lord's glory, are being transformed into
his image with ever-increasing glory, which
comes from the Lord, who is the Spirit.
(2 Corinthians 3:17-18, NIV)

11

Dental Student (IU) Missions

College Student Bible Study That Started at Home

There were 15 students in my very first class of IU School of Dentistry. My missionary focus at the college was to teach the Bible to the students. However, Bible study was strictly prohibited on campus. Although I felt inadequate to teach the Bible, I decided to start the Bible study at my home. I invited my students as well as Dr. Hyuntae Kim, a general surgeon commissioned from Campus Crusade for Christ (CCC), to give the gospel presentation. I invited him since he was very experienced in sharing the gospel. He came with 2 Cambodian staff members and shared the gospel through the Four Spiritual Laws. Leng Ravuth, one of the students who came for Bible study, accepted Jesus openly. Since Cambodia was a Buddhist country, it was very rare to see someone openly receiving Jesus. I felt very encouraged to see this at our first Bible study.

As I was teaching the Bible to the students at home, I felt so underqualified in many ways. I asked missionary Jim Stewart (a graduate of Westminster Seminary), whom I met at International Christian Fellowship (ICF), for help. He happily came to lead but I wasn't sure if his

Bible study was being translated properly in English (one student who was fluent in English translated for all the other students). So I asked missionary Sakal (Southern Baptist-commissioned Dallas Theological Seminary graduate) to come for translation.

Missionary Stewart preached on 2 Corinthians 3:17, "Now the Lord is the Spirit, and where the Spirit of the Lord is, there is freedom." After Jim's presentation of the gospel, Chum Chenda, one of the students, accepted Jesus as his Lord and Savior. It was such a thrilling moment. The powerful conviction of the Holy Spirit came upon Chenda and set him free from all the worldly chains. Since then, Chenda's faith continued to grow powerfully, and he is still serving his church with joy.

As time passed by, the students transitioned from working class to middle class. When they became more financially stable, they gradually lost interest in Bible study. They made excuses by saying their homes were far from the school and rejected my invitations. It was very disappointing to see that, because when they had less financial means, they

Missionary Jim Stewart (second row, third from left) and student Chum Chenda (first row, second from left)

would gladly come to my home, eat, and study the Bible together. At first, 6 or 7 students attended the Bible study. Then, it gradually decreased to 1 or 2 people. Even those 1-2 students probably came out of courtesy. However, one of the students who attended the Bible study, was Dr. Sopheak Ngor. He not only attended the Bible study, but also served as an interpreter. Today, he has a clinic in Sihanuk Ville.

Ivan Tardic's Cafe Restaurant

In the midst of those difficulties we faced in ministry, Dr. Ivan Tardic, a dental technician and a missionary from Germany, received a donation from a German church and was able to rent an entire building. He was teaching dental laboratory techniques at IU. We turned the first floor into a cafe and restaurant, and made a Bible study room on the second floor. When the students were invited again, many came to check out the new place.

Pastor Bong Ki Cho from Cambodia Presbyterian Theological In-

Professor Bong Ki Cho leading the Bible study

131

Missionary Ivan Tardic teaching dental techniques to Sam Pol

stitute came and led the Bible study. Pastor Cho even played the keyboard and led worship. He faithfully taught the Bible to about 10-12 students. He also spoke Cambodian very fluently.

At that time, the cafe restaurant needed a full-time manager, but Dr. Ivan had no time for that. Missionary McCullough from Canada had to manage the cafe. The cafe eventually went out of business as management wasn't going well and support money stopped coming in.

From a Cafe to a For-Profit Dental Clinic

After the cafe went out of business, we moved the Bible study room to our for-profit clinic that was nearby. Most of the Bible studies were led by Pastor Bong Ki Cho, but when Pastor Cho was on a sabbatical month, professor Yoon-Soo Lee of Cambodia Presbyterian Theological Institute came and taught the study. At these gatherings, not only did we teach the Bible but we also taught high-level dental techniques. We were effectively killing two birds with one stone. Many students came and benefited because they were able to learn the Bible and implant in one place. I challenged them by saying, "If you want to learn implant techniques from me, come to learn the Bible first." The students had the need to learn the implant techniques, so they came and studied the Bible as well.

After 4 years of ministry, Pastor Sakal went to study abroad to become a doctor. He went to Israel, instead of the United States, and got into a

Missionary Dave Everitt leading Bible study

medical school. He studied hard, but unfortunately, when he reached his senior year, he died of brain cancer. When Pastor Sakal passed away, his wife and their 4 children were having a hard time financially. She was an American. When they returned to Cambodia because of lower cost of living, I did my best to do the treatments for free.

The main lecturers of the Bible for the dental students were Pastor Bong Ki Cho and Dave Everitt. They consistently came and taught the Bible. After the Bible study, Dr. Makara taught about implants. In 2017, the last year before I retired, Dr. Makara and I taught the Bible study together. Mark Smith spoke Cambodian very fluently, but he was too busy. Then Dave Everitt came to lead Bible study.

First Sabbatical Year

On my first sabbatical year, starting December 2007, Dr. Leak obtained a dental license and came to know the Lord. When I was off on sabbatical, she took care of the dental clinic for the poor. She was so faithful with studying the Bible and managing the clinic. However, she contacted me and told me that she was resigning. That news of her resignation came as a huge surprise. Later we found out that she opened a clinic in her parents' building. She also stopped going to church and opened the clinic on Sundays to gain more patients. Dentists in Cambodia work even on Sundays, and as a result, dentists are not able to attend church on Sundays in order to treat their patients.

Dr. Leak is a very precious person that I met in Cambodia. She was one of 3 dental students that Dr. Chern Chern Choo had introduced to me. I taught them at the dental clinic from the fall semester of 2006 and also preached the gospel to them. Out of the 3, one of the students quit in the middle of the program, and another completed clinic and also participated in our portable dental missions. I took Dr. Leak to missionary Gil-hyun Kim's church and she got baptized there. Upon graduation, she began working as a full-time doctor at Tonle Basak Hospital's dental clinic. We had great collaboration as a team for 5 years.

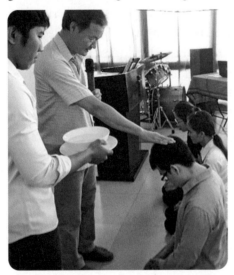

Missionary Kil-hyun Kim giving baptism to Dr. Eath. Deaconness Young Soon Choi from Inland Church had adopted Dr. Eath through the dental clinic ministry in Batambang. Ever since then, Young Soon Choi would pray for Dr. Eath during early dawn services. Upon my recommendation, Dr. Eath received Tres Dias training and his faith has grown considerably. He has become a mature believer now.

However, while Tina and I were back in the US for sabbatical, Dr. Leak sent the message of resignation. We tried to persuade her not to resign. However, she opened her own clinic and in order to survive from the competition with other clinics, she even opened her clinic on Sundays. Later, missionary Gil-hyun Kim and I visited her two or three times and strongly encouraged her to close the clinic and come to

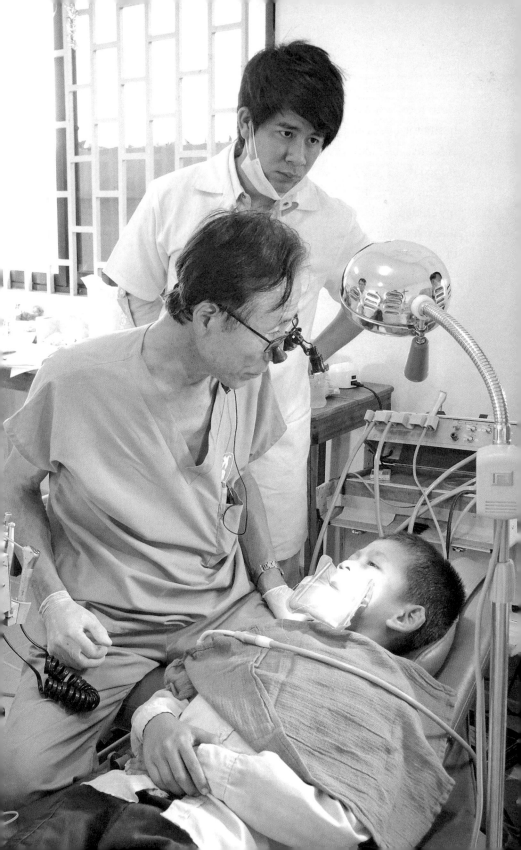

church on Sunday. However, she didn't listen. I am still praying earnestly for Dr. Leak to return to God. I still don't know what God's will is for her, but I am praying and convinced that she will return to God someday.

When I was in Cambodia, I attended The Way of Grace Church with my students, and missionary Gil-hyun Kim (former professor of pharmacy at Ewha Women's University). Pastor Kim was the senior pastor of the church.

Ehwa University in Seoul, Korea, was founded by missionary Mary F. Scranton, in 1886. Out of gratitude to Mrs. Scranton, Ehwa University

With the students from IU School of Dentistry, at Grace Korean Church, US

commissioned missionary Kim to come to Cambodia. Ehwa University also purchased a large piece of land from Srang village, Kampong Speu to build a preschool to college. Unfortunetly, Pastor Kim resigned. He was struggling under much responsibility, as he was building schools on the mountainside and trying to direct the construction process. He served faithfully for 10 years. Now the successor, Yoo Sun Kim, is doing an excellent job as the principal of the schools.

After quitting the construction process, missionary Gil-hyun Kim is focusing on building seminaries in Kampong Speu and raising future generations with financial support from LA Grace Korean Church. The seminary lectures were led by professors from LA. They also produced a lot of seminary students. Kim planted another church in front of the school in Srang village, and recently, he planted a church in Pailun, far from Phnom Penh and commissioned a local pastor to go there.

Durian, the King of Fruits

Durian is a tropical fruit that belongs to the Malvaceae family. It has an oval shape with a hard shell that is covered with sharp thorns. People who first encounter durian are usually shocked by its taste and powerful aroma. It is known for being banned at hotels for its horrible smell. However, those who like durian praise the taste and the scent of it and call it "the King of fruits." The taste is very strong and quite unique. My wife, Tina doesn't like durian, but it was my favorite fruit in Cambodia.

PART 4

To the Ends of the Earth

"

Although I am less than the least of all the Lord's people, this grace was given me: to preach to the Gentiles the boundless riches of Christ, and to make plain to everyone the administration of this mystery, which for ages past was kept hidden in God, who created all things His intent was that now, through the church, the manifold wisdom of God should be made known to the rulers and authorities in the heavenly realms, according to his eternal purpose that he accomplished in Christ Jesus our Lord. In him and through faith in him we may approach God with freedom and confidence (Ephesians 3:8-12, NIV).

12

The Difficulty of Leaving

Missionary David Koo

As I drew nearer to the end of my long-term missions work, my missions organization CRM began to actively look for my replacement. One of the potential candidates was missionary David Koo. He was a former dental surgeon in the United States Army. His father, his paternal grandfather, and even his maternal grandfather were all ordained ministers. This had a profound influence on David growing up, and

Missionary David Koo's family

as a result, his earliest yearning from childhood was to become a missionary. He had plenty of education, training, and experience in oral surgery and dental implants while he was in the army. Upon honorable discharge from his service in the army, Dr. Koo opened his own practice in Colorado Springs in 2009. At that time, Fullerton New Life Presbyterian Church focused solely on overseas missions to Cambodia. Dr. Koo came to Cambodia as a part of Fullerton New Life Presbyterian Church's short-term mission trip from Colorado Springs, and my mission team went and collaborated with them. It was at this time that missionary Koo accepted my recommendation to become my replacement and successor in Cambodia.

Unfortunately, due to difficult circumstances, missionary Koo served only for a year, from May 2016 to April 2017, and eventually went to Iraq with his family. During this one year period, missionary Koo served faithfully in the dental clinic, and allowed me to take time off to find my successor. Missionary Koo was in charge of the portable dental clinic ministry during that year, as well, and experienced a plethora of unique and diverse experiences in ministry.

One time, missionary Koo took our portable dental clinic to the Oddar Meanchey Province—a province located in the remote northwest of Cambodia where its long northern boundary demarcates part of Cambodia's border with Thailand. We travelled up there to work alongside a GDA missions team that had come from the United States. Missionary Koo's sister, who was an acupuncturist in Oriental medicine, also came. This was going to be the first exposure of this type of Oriental medicine in my portable medical/dental mission trips, so in my heart I was worried that no one would come and receive her treatment as we opened our portable dental clinic. My anxiety soon gave way to joy because the acupuncture treatments by missionary Koo's sister proved to be very effective in relieving pain. It did not take long for news to spread about the effectiveness of acupuncture/oriental medicine (AOM), and people started to flock to us and lines formed in order to receive the treatment. What a joyful and blessed memory that was!

Missionary Koo continues to do the same missions work in Iraq. I firmly believe that God sent missionary Koo and his family to Cambodia in order to train and prepare him for the kind of missions work that he was to do in Iraq. When it comes to the work that God does, not a single moment of time or effort goes

Sister of missionary Koo giving acupuncture to a Buddhist monk.

to waste; He orchestrates all things to advance His kingdom. Many things happen in our lives, maybe a series of events that unfold unexpectedly which baffle our minds. Nonetheless, when we obey God and His will in those unfathomable moments, we begin to see why God allowed those things to happen in our lives. And in hindsight, such events reveal the mystery of God's will, to which we thank and praise God. Just as the Apostle Paul praised God for the Ephesian church during his imprisonment for the "mystery of His will according to His good pleasure, which he purposed in Christ" (Eph. 1:9, NIV), likewise we must in all things acknowledge Him and praise Him.

"Although I am less than the least of all the Lord's people, this grace was given me: to preach to the Gentiles the boundless riches of Christ, and to make plain to everyone the administration of this mystery, which for ages past was kept hidden in God, who created all things" (Ephesians 3:8-9, NIV).

In order to meet the financial goal that the CRM mission department had set, missionary Koo was doing his best to raise financial support for his mission. By this time, missionary Koo and his family were in Hawaii, receiving training at the University of Nations. Soon afterwards, missionary Koo expressed his desire to receive field training, not in Cambodia but to Iraq. Upon this news, I appealed to missionary Koo that since he had already committed to Cambodia long term, to consider bringing his entire family to experience Cambodia. As decisions and appeals went back and forth, the CRM mission department gave missionary Koo an ultimatum—either to decide on going to Cambodia or to Iraq, but to make a decision and follow through with it. Ultimately, missionary Koo decided to go to Iraq with Youth With A Mission (YWAM) as a dentist. Currently, missionary Koo is doing ministry in the refugee camps in the Kurdistan region of Iraq.

I introduced missionary David Koo to Pohang Daehung Church (Pastor Heungbin Lee) as my successor. This church had officially decided to support missionary Koo as my replacement in overseas missions to Cambodia. In the end, missionary Koo decided to go to Iraq through YWAM, a mission organization that we did not have a partnership with. Nonetheless, as the Apostle states in Philippians, in every way the gospel of Jesus Christ is proclaimed! To this day, Pohang Daehung Church continues to financially support David Koo in his missionary work in Iraq

In July 2017, missionary Koo arrived in the Kurdistan region of Iraq and started to help the Syrian refugees in the refugee camps through portable dental clinics. Missionary Koo currently resides in Dohuk, the capital of the Dohuk Governorate in Iraq's Kurdistan region, teaching at a college of dentistry. Dohuk is located 50 kilometers north of Mosul and 100 kilometers northwest of Erbil. In 2018, missionary Koo moved to Jordan for his children's education. He continued to help the Syrian refugees from Jordan, helping and treating the refugees with his portable dental clinic. Even now, missionary Koo is continuing the ministry of teaching at the Kurdistan dental university once every other month. God led missionary Koo to be a dental missionary in order to bring the gospel of Jesus to hard-to-reach Islamic areas, which would have been difficult for normal, traditional missionaries. Now he plans to return to Kurdistan.

Relocation of Dental Clinic to Mercy Medical Center (MMC)

Even to this day, my heart yearns and prays for not only dental clinics in general, but also for the dental clinics serving the poor and underprivileged. Starting in the middle of 2016, Mercy Medical Center (MMC), formerly a Southern Baptist Cooperative Services International (CSI) clinic, began operating under the leadership of its new medical director Dr. Timothy Benadum. There was a sharp decline in financial support from the International Mission Board of the Southern Baptist Convention. The numbers of Southern Baptist missionary shrinked to one-third of them. With my missionary service scheduled to complete at the end of 2017, I began to work with the hospital director of MMC in order to hand over the dental clinic, the mission hub for our ministry to the underprivileged and the poor. I signed an affidavit of agreement stating that: (1) I would hand over all the dental equipment to MMC free of charge, and (2) Dr. Buntha, a dentist who worked under me full time in the MMC, would be entrusted as the head of the dental department. Therefore, per our agreement, on December 1, 2016, Dr. Buntha and a few nurses became official employees at the Mercy Dental Center.

Unfortunately, after only a year, Dr. Buntha informed me that he would be resigning from his post at the Mercy Dental Center. Apparently, there was a sharp disagreement and dissension between Dr. Buntha and hospital director Dr. Timothy Benadum. Upon hearing what had happened, I strongly recommended and urged Dr. Buntha to continue working at the dental clinic because he played a part in the conflict with the dental clinic as well. When the situation did not get better, I turned to the missionary who had introduced and connected me to Dr. Buntha—missionary Peter Kong. After he met with Dr. Buntha, missionary Kong explained that, upon hearing what had happened, it would be impossible for Dr. Buntha to continue working at the dental clinic. Missionary Kong advised me to allow Dr. Buntha to resign and leave the dental clinic. Missionary Kong had a great understanding of the Cambodian culture. It was only after hearing the cultural background and advice from missionary Kong that I began to comprehend what Dr. Buntha was feeling. But this created quite a predicament for Dr. Buntha. He had received a scholarship that had a requirement; that is, in order to receive this scholarship, Dr. Buntha had to work 3 years more at a dental missions agency or return the scholarship in its entirety. This was the qualification and agreement arranged beforehand with the mission organization. As a result, we were deeply worried for Dr. Buntha in his predicament. It so happened that at this time, missionary Byung Seol Chung, who specialized in mobile dental clinics, came from Canada. Missionary Chung said that he was in need of a dentist and nurses for his ministry! I immediately introduced Dr. Buntha to missionary Chung. In the past, I had connected and recommended dental doctors to missionary Chung. Those same doctors continued to minister and work together with missionary Chung in his mobile dental clinic. Missionary Chung welcomed Dr. Buntha, who had vast dental experience, with open arms. Dr. Buntha is continuing to work with missionary Chung even to this day.

After Dr. Buntha left the Mercy Dental Center to join missionary Chung, the Mercy Dental Center was unable to find a Christian dentist to lead the dentistry. As a result, Dr. Timothy Benadum had to remove all the dental equipment and established an optometry department instead. All the dental equipment that was purchased was brand new and very expensive. Therefore, it is such a shame and unfortunate that all this precious dental equipment had to be removed and put in storage. I pray earnestly that a dentistry for the underprivileged and the poor can open again as soon as possible, Lord willing.

Dr. Makara, Dental Director

I did my best to advertise, contact, and recruit missionaries who could be my replacement in the mission field for both the non-profit and for-profit dental clinics. After a long search, I was unable to find a Christian dentist. Instead, I handed over the for-profit dental clinic to Dr. Makara as the manager, and Dr. Chen Pagna as an assistant dentist. Dr. Makara and Dr. Pagna calculated all the costs of equipment and dental supplies and reimbursed with cash to InnerCHANGE. Dr. Chen Pagna, a Christian dentist, was my former student at IU. Dr. Makara was someone that I deeply respected. I was able to leave Cambodia in peace because I knew that the dental clinic was in good hands with

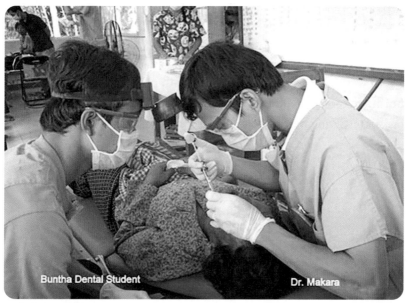

Buntha Dental Student   Dr. Makara

Dr. Makara (right) treating a patient

Dr. Makara. Even to this day, Dr. Makara is managing the for-profit dental clinic well. Unfortunately, the Mercy Medical Center, which was the dental clinic for the underprivileged and poor, is still waiting for a missionary who could relaunch the dental ministry. I pray earnestly that the Lord may send a great and dedicated dental missionary to the Mercy Dental Center.

After serving in Cambodia for 14 years, we returned to our home in the United States. In May of 2018, I returned to the IU in Cambodia to teach my last lecture for 6th year class. I stayed in Cambodia for the next 5 months (May to September). On October 2, 2018, my dental missions in Cambodia officially came to an end. With my wife, Tina, who is not only the love of my life but also my friend and co-worker in the Lord, we finished 14 years of dental missions in Cambodia together, and returned to the United States.

Oh my beloved Cambodia! We give all the glory and thanksgiving and honor to our Lord Jesus Christ for using such an insufficient and inadequate family as ours to serve in and for Cambodia for those 14 years!

"However, I consider my life worth nothing to me; my only aim is to finish the race and complete the task the Lord Jesus has given me—the task of testifying to the good news of God's grace" (Acts 20:24, NIV).

EXPERIENCING CAMBODIAN CULTURE

Mango

Mango from Cambodia is the best in the world. This mango from Cambodia, commonly known as the "normal mango," is harvested in May. Don't let the name fool you however. Even though the Cambodian mango is quite common and produced in great quantity, the mango that is imported to the United States from South America does not even compare to the taste and quality of the "normal mango" from Cambodia. The best mango in both quality and quantity is no doubt the "svay chun " mango. This is a close-up of the pale yellow cucumber seed. The sweet yet fragrant taste of the svay chun is considered the best even by the locals, often used and purchased as a high-end gift. The small "square mango" is green inside has a very peculiar taste. The locals make salads out of the "square mango" when it is not ripe yet. When the mango is not ripe, the insides are white and very hard. Lastly, the small "round mango" is an orange mango which has a sweet and sour taste. Even to this day, the scent and the taste of Cambodian mangos make me happy!

"
I thank my God every time I remember you. In all my prayers for all of you, I always pray with joy because of your partnership in the gospel from the first day until now, being confident of this, that He who began a good work in you will carry it on to completion until the day of Christ Jesus (Philippians 1:3-6, NIV).

13

My Beloved
Co-Workers

There were people who were so precious to partner with such inadequate people like us, who helped share God's love towards Cambodia. If I did not have such fellow co-workers in Jesus Christ, my ministry in Cambodia would have been extremely difficult and arduous. If not for these co-workers, the ray of the light of God's love would not have shown nearly as brightly to the marginalized. As I look back on the 14 years of ministry in Cambodia, I want to reflect on and remember my dear friends, co-workers, and mentors in the mission field.

1. Team Leader Mark and Susan Smith

On August 6, 2004, my wife and I finally arrived at Phnom Penh, the capital city of Cambodia. The first thing that overtook us was the humid and oppressive heat. Then and there, my wife and I truly felt what it was like to live in a tropical country like Cambodia.

Team leader missionary Mark Smith and his wife, Susan, had come to greet us at the airport. They took us to a small hotel located near a river in the city, and from there, they actively helped us find a suitable place for us to live in the city. It was the policy of InnerCHANGE, the mission organization that we were affiliated with, for its members to live within the city they were doing ministry.

The team that my wife and I were a part of was composed of 6 families and 3 single missionaries. Our team leader Mark Smith

Missionary Mark and Susan Smith's family

was from Baltimore, Maryland, Dave Everitt from Colorado Springs, Colorado, and Heap Him was a native of Cambodia who had married a caucasian wife from Maine. All these families in our team were senior, veteran missionaries who had been in Cambodia for a while.

Yong Lim was a single male missionary from Florida. He was a computer expert who played a pivotal role with us in our ministry. Hayden Swerl was a single male missionary from central Arkansas. He arrived as a part of our team at the same time as us. Diane Moss was a single female missionary from Atlanta. She was one of the senior, veteran missionaries, who was in charge of the AIDS rehabilitation program in the city of Kampong Cham. Chris Even was from Malvern, Australia, and his wife, Samantha was from Central California. Before she was married, Samatha worked in a homeless ministry in San Francisco. At the InnerCHANGE (IC), Samantha operated a shelter where people could take showers and provided food for them. Samantha would sometimes even sleep next to the homeless people and shared the gospel with them! Danny Colombara and his wife, Anita came to Cambodia 6 months before we did. Danny and his family along with Chris and Hayden were living around our team leader Mark. They were passionately and fervently studying the Cambodian language. The name of the slum town within the city of Phnom Penh where our team was ministering was called Boeing Trabek. The town was so under-developed that there was not even one road for a car to drive on. Because his children were attending elementary school, David was living in a nicer location nearby. Since my wife and I were a lot older, we were able to live right across the street from missionary David and his family.

Our team leader Mark was a great person with great character, who was also well-educated and had this amazing ability to teach the Bible in such a simple and understandable way. Mark was fluent in the Cambodian language, and as a result, Mark preached and taught the Word of God every Sunday at a local Cambodian church. His wife, Susan, was also fluent in Cambodian and ministered alongside her husband in teaching the local women. Furthermore, Susan also helped lead our mission team.

As the team leader, Mark took care of any work or issues that were related to the Cambodian government. His duties, which were very difficult, were the following: team visa issues and renewal; the report

InnerCHANGE mission team members

153

and permit for the AIDS rehabilitation center; and permits that had to be renewed every 3 years. It was not an easy task to be in charge of handling all the government documentations, guidelines, and officials. Government officials and administrators, for no apparent reason, would give us a difficult time by making things harder than they were supposed to. Mark was in Cambodia for a very long time, a veteran missionary, and therefore, had great relationships with missionaries from other mission organizations. Whenever we were in difficult situations, we would always turn to Mark for his advice and received his help many times in our ministry.

Mark's wife, Susan, taught us ways to avoid and prevent diarrhea, malaria, and the dengue virus and fever. Mark was frequently traveling abroad in order to attend the meetings for the mission headquarters as well as the leadership meetings for the Asia region. Whenever he gave orientations and training for the new interns, Mark always emphasized that 85 percent of people in Cambodia are Buddhists, and in order to evangelize to such people, we must know and understand Buddhism, as well. He explained the difference between Mahayana and Hinayana Buddhism, and since Cambodia follows Hinayana Buddhism, Mark went into depths concerning this branch of Buddhism. He warned the interns not to have a condescending attitude towards Buddhism when introducing the genuine truth of Christianity. Furthermore, Mark made it mandatory for team members to take 4 to 5 days off once a year in order to rest physically, to focus on personal devotional time, and to reflect on spiritual and mental health for our ministry. This helped us to realign ourselves spiritually and to recharge. Although we take 2 weeks off once a year for vacation, Mark strongly recommended that we not go back to America but instead visit neighboring countries near Cambodia. He only allowed travel to the United States during our sabbatical year. On top of this, Mark strongly urged that if ministry became too busy to the point where you could not even take time to do personal devotions or even go on vacation, then we had to set down everything immediately and go on a vacation to recharge and to realign. In fact, every year, our mission headquarters would send a clinical psychologist missionary in order to provide marital relationship counseling as well as other areas of counseling. Our team leader Mark was a relatively young man, 14 years ago. His mustache really fit him well. Now, as he has entered into his 60s, Mark's hair has thinned out a bit. As the popular saying goes, "You cannot outrun Father Time." As I look back, I can confidently say that from the beginning to the end of my ministry in Cambodia, the love and support that I received from Mark did not change at all. I will never forget Mark's sacrificial service. Mark is still serving as the team leader in Cambodia, serving ever so faithfully as a laborer for God and His Kingdom.

2. Missionary David and Lisa Everitt

David and Lisa were veteran missionaries who came to Cambodia in 1996. Both of them were very active, bright, and showed a strong affinity for others. David was one of the founding members of the mission hospital for Cooperative Services International (CSI). Since we lived very close to the Everitt family and served in the same hospital, we became very close with them. Since he was

Missionary Lisa teaching how to brush teeth

fluent in Khmer, David actively managed local employees serving as janitors, security guards, etc. Once every other month, David would go into remote villages in order to evangelize. He would take his motorcycle with these huge wheels because cars were unable to drive in those remote places! David would carry his enormous first aid backpack while he evangelized. When he would find a person in need of medical assistance, David would provide emergency treatment and arranged for the medical clinicization of patients. In doing so, David put the love of Christ into practice.

His wife, Lisa was very good at administration and organization. She was so good that when our team leader Mark Smith was gone for 5 years as the executive director of InnerCHANGE, Lisa took over many of Mark's responsibilities as the team leader. Before the main medical/dental team would enter the remote village that David was in charge of, David would ride his motorcycle ahead into the village in order to prepare and to help the main team. While the patients were waiting for their diagnosis and treatment, David's wife Lisa would first share the gospel of Jesus Christ and then share the proper way to brush and floss.

David and Lisa returned to America in 2016 for their sabbatical. During this time, they changed the direction and focus of their missions and began working in refugee camps in Oregon, seeking to do ministry in Jordan or Near East. Unfortunately, God did not open the doors to either of those places. As a result, David went back to Cambodia in 2019 and has continued the itinerant evangelism ministry that he was doing before. Naming his ministry the "Prayer Circle," David is still riding his big motorcycle and traveling around the country, sharing the good news of Jesus. Twice a year, after forming a team of missionaries and locals who can ride motorcycles, David goes around the country, doing the "Prayer Circle" ministry. David attended Near East mission conference in Dubai, traveling 35 hours by plane riding one way from the US.

At the for-profit dental clinic, David taught the Bible first to dental students before implant study. During this time, David would take turns with missionary Yewon to lead 30-minute Bible studies. When I was leading this 30-minute Bible study, I felt so limited in what I could convey because I had to have Dr. Makara as my translator. David, on the other hand, proved to be very effective because he was able to communicate fluently in Cambodian. I had initially asked my team leader Mark to lead Bible study, but he was unable to do so because of his busy schedule. On Mark's behalf, David took up the task and we saw abundant fruit from his Bible studies. I give the utmost praise and glory to Jesus Christ for allowing us to meet and work alongside David and Lisa. Currently, David is preparing to go to Turkey. Just recently, David received a vision, "Go to Turkey," while he was praying, and now, he is preparing for a vision trip to Turkey.

3. Missionary Yong Lim

Missionary Yong Lim was a refugee when he was young, but came to the United States and grew up near Jacksonville in Florida. After majoring in computer science, Yong was working for a company when God called him to go to Cambodia as a missionary. Yong particularly loved the portable dental ministry, and therefore, considered it to be an important part of his ministry. Before the portable medical/dental clinic went into a new town, it was missionary Yong's responsibility to go into that particular town a month before in order to research and look into potential lodging and potential locations that were suitable for the medical/dental clinic to operate with an adequate power source and electricity for all the equipment. On the day that the portable medical/dental clinic would begin travelling to the site, missionary Yong would take his motorcycle and ride ahead and meet us at the location. Missionary Yong was our tech support for anything related to computers. Whenever BAM (Business as Missions) missionaries or Christian schools had issues and problems with their computers, missionary Yong would always go and fix the problem.

Being tall and strong, Yong would help move the heavy equipment in the portable dental clinic. Yong would always be with me and help me determine what kind of treatment patients would need because he speaks Khmer. Yong always took initiative with every and any kind of work in the ministry. My wife, Tina was very grateful for Yong because he would help Tina with the computer whenever she had to write up reports. Missionary Yong was an indispensable and valuable resource—a person whom we really needed in our ministry. Furthermore, missionary Yong taught English at the Light and Salt middle and high school. Operated by a Korean missionary, the Light and Salt school was a boarding school that provided outstanding education for the children of Cambodian pastors who were ministering in remote villages. This school had difficulty finding an English teacher, so when they reached out to me, I connected missionary Yong to the school and he taught English for 4 years at this school. In 2018, missionary Yong met and married Wendy, a British nurse who was working at the Mercy Medical Center. Yong and Wendy are happily married and enjoying ministry together.

I want to share what missionary Yong recently shared with me. He wrote, "With the outbreak of COVID-19 pandemic, I have been inundated with requests from schools for help as they transition to an online classroom setting. Since my outings have increased, way more than usual, I am exposed to danger more and more. Before all this madness, I had taught myself and learned Zoom and Google Classroom simply because of my personal interest. I would have never even imagined in my wildest dreams that such a worldwide pandemic like COVID-19 would ever happen! It is amazing how God was preparing me for things without me knowing it. Please pray for me that God will protect me and give me strength."

4. Missionary Hayden Swerl

In August of 2004, Hayden was a single missionary who had received two weeks of InnerCHANGE mission training in San Francisco with my wife and me. We had all come to Cambodia together after the training. After working in Hanoi, Vietnam, with the Mennonite Missions for 4 years, Hayden came to InnerCHANGE. Hayden was always adventurous. During our early days of learning the Cambodian language, Hayden volunteered himself to live in a remote village, away from the city, with an elderly couple who lived in a very shabby house made of wood. He stayed there for over a month—eating the same food as the locals, sleeping there, and learning their language and culture. They did not even have working telephones. But Hayden, ventured in with only his camera equipment. Taking pictures was one of Hayden's passions. Therefore, he would always grab his good camera, a reflective umbrella, and another camera for videography. Honestly, his equipment looked better than most small photo studios! Hayden had created many videos. One of the videos he made was "The Good Samaritan." He got many of the local young adults to get involved in the short film, and even asked me to play the role of a high priest! Although I only had a minor role in this short film, I was so joyful to be given the opportunity to be an actor. Hayden's films were very useful during our missions. Those are pleasant and heart-warming memories.

Hayden also had an eye for making brochures. He even made the brochure for the ADC Lab (established by missionary William Hur). ADC Lab still uses Hayden's pictures from the brochure even to this day. In fact, a local doctor took Hayden's pictures from the brochure and posted them on his dental clinic windows as a way of advertising. Hayden is currently in the United Arab Emirates, ministering to foreign construction workers. Hayden was such a faithful and dependent co-worker in the Lord!

5. Single Missionary Lynn Ogata

Lynn Ogata, Ph.D. of immunology, was a single missionary from Seattle, Washington, in the United States. She was working as a doctor of immunology before she become a missionary. Lynn was a part of another mission organization, but had later joined with NOVO and began to minister to the poor and the underprivileged.

Dr. Lynn shared the gospel with Cambodian youth through her Onyx program and Dove Cambodia program. Dr. Lynn would plan outdoor retreats where she not only taught English but also uplifted the

Missionary Lynn Ogata

spirituality of the Cambodian youth. When I asked Dr. Lynn to recommend someone to work at my for-profit dental clinic, she recommended Pov, a young lady, a computer programmer through the Onyx program. Srey Pov spoke English very well with an American accent, so she was able to communicate quite well with the American missionaries and worked extremely hard as the receptionist.

Dr. Lynn is still working at the IC. Dr. Lynn's home church, Seattle Presbyterian Church, donated funds to build 110 thatched houses in the poorest village of Andong. Dr. Lynn was a sincere and faithful co-worker in the Lord.

6. Missionary Trish and Anthony

Anthony was a young missionary working as an administrator in the Southern Baptist's International Mission Board. At that time, many missionaries were working in Cooperative Services International (CSI) as well as operating the mission dental clinic. Administrative tasks and responsibilities were overwhelming. Dental missionaries who were working in the dental clinic had to renew their visas every 2 years. For the approved non-governmental organizations (NGOs), visas were free. The visa fee was normally $250 per year per family, which was quite expensive! But whenever short-term medical/dental mission teams would come from the United States, they brought a lot of medicines and equipment. As a result, these teams had to receive permission from the Cambodian Customs Department ahead of time. This was important because only with official permission could we document it to CSI as a part of our mission report. It was an extremely arduous task to obtain official permission from customs every single time. In each instance, Anthony had to go to the Customs Department in person, wait all day, and finally receive the official permit from the administrative officials right before the Customs office closed at 5 p.m. The reason why it was so difficult for us to receive permits for equipment and medicine the team brought because we did not offer any money (bribes) to the officials. Missionary Tony (that was what we called Anthony) also ministered to the ethnic group of Cham people in the Kampong Cham Province.

We were indebted to missionary Tony numerous times. We would drop off our passports to Tony in his office every 2 years and he would go to the Ministry of Foreign Affairs, go through all the procedures, and receive our visas and bring them back to our office. On top of this, I had to submit dental ministry plans as well as financial documents (expenditure and budget) to the Cambodian government every 3years. This was mandatory and necessary in order to continue my dental mission work in Cambodia. This was not an easy task, to say the least! Together with Tony, I had to carefully write down and organize all the dental clinic budget expenses, mission work's expenses as well as the value of the portable dental clinic in great detail. What was really tedious was assessing work's financial value of all the medical/dental work we provided, and converting it to US dollars. I would not have been able to go through this meticulous and strenuous process of writing up these government documents if it was not for Tony. As our administrator, Tony took care of all this meticulous work. I will never forget all his hard work. As of now, Tony is ministering in a country that I cannot name, because it is a closed country. I believe that he is now over 50 years old.

7. Dr. Tom Love

I first met Dr. Tom Love in 2003 at the Christian Dental Society (CDS) board of directors meeting in San Francisco. Dr. Love had a dental clinic in Oakland in Northern California, and was known as a specialist in oral surgery. The board of directors in San Francisco had convened in order to judge and decide whether I would be qualified to be sent out as a missionary to Cambodia. Dr. Love was one of

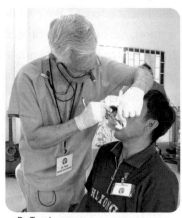

Dr. Tom Love

the board members. During this meeting, Dr. Love actively supported me in being commissioned to Cambodia. The only thing that Dr. Love required from me was to send back a financial report every 3 months.

When I arrived in Cambodia in late 2005, I started my portable dental clinic and as agreed upon, I began to submit my financial reports to the CDS board of directors. As a board member, Tom would read my reports. After finishing dental missions in Vietnam in 2006, Tom came to Cambodia for a week in order to join and to help with the portable dental clinic. After this, Dr. Love came every year. Sometimes, all the way from America, Tom came twice a year. So many people who knew him were so moved and grateful for his fiery passion—to the point that whenever Tom came out to help, upon his recommendation, he would bring so many doctors that he knew with him! Among the doctors that came with Tom were Dr. Tom Dowling from Wisconsin and Dr. Matt Lui from San Francisco, who for 2 years came with Tom to Cambodia to help. Upon his recommendation, Kathleen, a medical nurse, also came to Cambodia to help for 2 consecutive years. Portable medical/dental clinic not only needs a dentist but also a general medical doctor. A general medical doctor needed at least one person to see medical patients. There are so many people needing medical care in the country, and therefore, we need a nurse as well.

Every time he came, Dr. Tom Love would bring his own personal, specialized tools with him in 2 plastic boxes. All the patients who needed tooth extraction were sent to Dr. Love, and he handled them so effectively and efficiently. Using his special tools that he brought, Dr. Love was able to demonstrate his extraordinary skill by extracting even the most difficult of teeth—the wisdom tooth—so quickly and effectively. He would get 7 to 8 patients to sit next to each other in a row and would do the anesthesia all at once. Then, Dr. Love would extract the patients' teeth one by one. This swift and effective method was so admirable! There was one occasion when, using this method, Dr. Love took care of nearly 100 patients in a single day! Dr. Love allowed other dentists to focus on other patients whose teeth were redeemable. Sometimes, Dr. Love's wife, Holly, a woman of great faith, would come to help him, despite having a medical condition that caused swelling in both of her legs.

One of the years, upon Tom's recommendation, the Vets With A Mission (VWAM) team came to Cambodia instead of going to Vietnam as planned. The VWAM was a very large medical team. With the VWAM medical team, we treated

Dr. Tom Love and his wife, Holly.

patients in the Floating Village and its surrounding rural villages in the Siem Reap Province and spent the last two days treating patients in an area near the Cambodian-Thai border. This was done through cooperation with Pastor Sitan, a well-known pastor in Cambodia as well as my dental team.

The Floating Village was the residence of the Vietnamese people who had moved to Cambodia a long time ago. Since they had no land, they would make their living by fishing in rivers and lakes nearby. In particular, Tonle Sap Lake, the largest freshwater lake in all of Southeast Asia, is full of floating villages and a diverse ecosystem. The people living in these floating villages have been there for generations and still use Vietnamese to communicate with one another. The floating villages are complete with floating schools, medical clinics, banks, churches, restaurants, and tourist shops.

Dr. Love taught the importance of spending time with God after enjoying dinner and a full day of ministry. He emphasized to the team the importance of reflecting upon the ministry we had done in order to not only identify the problems but to come up with solutions to those problems. Not only that, Dr. Love taught us to celebrate our successes and encourage one another, as well as spending time with God in prayer to ask for His direction and help. We cannot forget Dr. Love's fervent faith, passion, and his love for Cambodia. I want to give our thanks and highest esteem to Dr. Tom Love for being there for us, working with us, and really guiding us from beginning to end. We thank the Lord for His grace in sending Dr. Tom Love to us. Let me briefly introduce Dr. Tom Love. He enlisted in the Navy at the age of 17 where he was a military medic for the Navy Marine Corps. He was stationed at Marine Corps Base Camp Pendleton in San Diego. After his honorable discharge, Dr. Tom Love entered dental school to become a dentist and finished his residency at Michigan University and opened a dentistry specializing in oral surgery. Dr. Love served as the Director of the Vets With a Mission

(VWAM) where he went back to Vietnam every year for 2 to 3 weeks in order to treat patients. Since Cambodia was right next to Vietnam, I think that this piqued Dr. Love's interest towards Cambodia. According to the latest news I received from him, Dr. Tom is near the end of his 51-year career of oral surgery. Dr. Tom told me that it was solely the grace of God that he was able to visit 20 countries on 80 different dental missions. Furthermore, Dr. Tom informed me that next year he will visit the refugee camps in the Middle East and dentists in West Africa in order to teach them for a week on how to use battery-operated dental equipment for removing impacted teeth.

8. My Precious Co-worker, Missionary Kisoo Hwang

Missionary Hwang lived in the town behind the Chinese Embassy in Phnom Penh for a long time. He lived with 5-6 college students in his long and narrow, 4m x 15m, 3-story house. There, he taught the

Missionary Kisoo Hwang with his wife missionary Sinja Chun.

Bible to the students and prayed with them every day at early dawn. This is called a bachelors ministry. He faithfully served the students through bachelors ministry for many years, raising them as Sunday school teachers, seminary students, and men of faith.

Among them, there was one student whom Hwang cherished the most: Sei Ha. Missionary Hwang named him David. Hwang had a grand vision to raise him as a future pastor and a pillar of their denomination. Hwang wanted to send David to Westminster Seminary in Philadelphia, so he asked me to introduce an American missionary. I introduced missionary Hayden to David to meet frequently after school to practice English. David studied the Bible diligently every day. Whenever Hwang and David got into the car in the morning to leave the house, if Hwang forgot to pray, David would remind him to pray before they left. Although David wanted to go to the US to study, it was so hard to obtain the visa.

Eventually, he gave up on going to Westminster Seminary and changed directions to South Korea. However, as he was waiting for the acceptance letter from Korea, he crossed the line with a female student who he was studying the Bible together with. The female student was sent from a local pastor and was also serving as a Sunday School teacher every week. Missionary Hwang found out what happened through the confession of the female student, so he urged David to marry her. However, David refused to marry the girl because of the large educational gap they had. Hwang was very disappointed and discouraged and David eventually left the house. For someone who loved and cherished David and desired to raise him as a faithful servant of God, this incident was like a broken dream. We were also very embarrassed and sad to watch what happened. The sexual morality of Cambodian society is relatively low. Many husbands leave their wives and children for other women. Because the sexual morality of the culture is still weak, Cambodian society is very lenient about sexual immorality.

Let me briefly introduce the ministry of missionary Hwang. As a part of his ministry to the undergraduates, missionary Hwang would lead Bible study in his home in 2004. One of his students in Bible study was an elementary teacher. This elementary teacher, then, introduced him to a kindergarten teacher by the name of Chanton. This was no ordinary encounter—by meeting Chanton, God has allowed missionary Hwang to go to a new phase in his ministry. The place that Chanton worked as a teacher was Takeo. Takeo was about 90 minutes away from Phnom Penh and the place that he worked was called Phum Thmei (New Village). This particular village was a traditional Cambodian village where the people made silk through sericulture as well as farming. Unlike the village of Khmer, this old town had a strong economy.

At that time, the elementary school principal, as well as the affluent people from the town of Phum Thmei, decided to establish a kindergarten within the school. This pointed to the stability of this rural commune. Unfortunately, the rich people from the town did not pay what they promised and the preschool went into financial difficulty. That is why Chanton asked missionary Hwang for help. After visiting the town, missionary Hwang thought the town would be a great place for his ministry. Hwang saw a vision of the preschool and decided to help Chanton with the management and building extension. Chanton was actually a good Christian. After missionary Hwang expanded the preschool facilities through renovation and hired more teachers, finally, a proper kindergarten was born.

Through all this, missionary Hwang became good friends with the principal and some of the teachers. Through those relationships, Hwang was able to bring them and the affluent people of the town and start a Bible study. He prioritized this Bible study every Thursday and did not hesitate to drive a very long distance. When the high school students from that town went to college, he would take them into his bachelor house, teach them the Bible and take care of them. In 2011, Hwang started receiving support from First Presbyterian Church in Philadelphia (his home church) and purchased a piece of land. In 2013, he received support from Masan Church in Korea and built a kindergarten (Sunday school on Sundays). In 2016, he invited the senior pastor from First Presbyterian Church in Philadelphia and let him baptize 36 seniors who had been a part of his Bible study. After that, missionary Hwang established an official church and named it Bethel Garden Church. Children would worship in the morning and the adults worshipped in the afternoon. In 2016, he purchased 40m x 90m land located behind the kindergarten and built the main sanctuary in

2018. The inaugural service was conducted in 2019.

Our dental team also visited this town 3 times and helped missionary Hwang's ministry. Missionary Hwang really liked the portable dental mission. Missionary Hwang wanted to help the villagers since there was no proper dental facility or financial, emotional stability. Our team wanted to help missionary Hwang in every way possible. Even in 2020, Dr. Makara had a dental mission planned for June with missionary Hwang. It was scheduled because of missionary Hwang's earnest request. For me to go back to this place would have been very meaningful! The Bethel Garden Church was blessed to have 36 adult farmers and young adults who were baptized.

Since I retired, Dr. Makara has been using his own money to go on portable dental missions. However, it is very sad to hear that all the dental missions and worship services have been prevented due to COVID-19. Since Buddhist culture is deeply rooted in Cambodian culture, it is very hard to evangelize adults. For that reason, most of the church plantings are targeted at young students and only about 2-3 families. However, Hwang's ministry at Bethel Garden Church in Phum Thmei was so blessed, as God sent so many older adults and young students at the same time

Missionary Kisoo Hwang was my spiritual leader and a good missionary partner. Missionary Hwang and his wife do not have a home to return to in America. With overflowing love and devotion towards Cambodia, Hwang desires to live in Cambodia until the Lord calls him to his heavenly home. All glory and honor to the Lord!

9. The First Korean Missionary, Chang Yoon Kang

The first thing that I did when I arrived in Cambodia was to look for Korean missionaries. It so happened that I met missionary Chang Yoon Kang who happened to live on the same block as I did. Missionary Kang was serving at the Phum Marl Church, which was located in

the suburbs of Phnom Penh towards the killing fields. When I
attended this church, there were
many adults and it looked like a
very solid church. When I asked
missionary Kang for recommen-
dations on potential employees,
he recommended Sovan Kol Yee
and Sovanny. Sovan Kol is currently the laboratory manager.
Sovanny is still working as dental assistant in ADC. When Leng

*Missionary Chang Yoon Kang with his wife
missionary Ji Ok Joo.*

Chan Heng moved near the Phum Marl Church, I recommended her to
check the church out. Leng Chan Heng's faith grew tremendously there
and she received evangelism training. Now, she is going out regularly to
share the gospel of Jesus Christ.

Here is the story of how missionary Kang is honored came to Cambodia as the first Korean missionary. For a very long time, missionary
Kang wanted to go to China for missions. However, the door to China
did not open for him until he graduated from seminary. When he was
receiving mission training in his denomination (Hapdong Reformed),
he heard about recruiting for missionaries to Cambodia. However,
he did not apply to be a missionary to Cambodia because he heard
that there were no Korean missionaries there. Towards the end of his
1-year mission training, he received a call from the mission department stating that there are still no missionaries to Cambodia. There
were no applicants because Cambodia was at war at that time. He said,
"I was struggling with the idea of going to Cambodia or not, but at that
moment, I remembered an old hymn that I used to sing. There's a line
in that hymn that says, 'I am willing to go.'" Remembering this hymn,
missionary Kang made the decision to obey God's will if He wanted

him to go.

Missionary Kang informed the mission department that he would go to Cambodia only if his future wife agreed to go to Cambodia with him. To his surprise, missionary Kang's future wife, who did not know where Cambodia was even located, agreed to go with him. Therefore, in October of 1992, missionary Kang married his wife and they were sent off as missionaries to Cambodia by their denomination. Missionary Kang and his wife spent their honeymoon in Cambodia, and after that, in January of 1993, they moved to Cambodia, and till now, are serving as missionaries.

Recently, missionary Kang shared about the sad and painful reality of the Cambodian church.

He wrote, "One of the hardest things that I experienced here in Cambodia is that the people who claim to believe in Jesus actually do not really know Jesus. In its infancy, the Cambodian church was established through the fervent mission work of non-profit organizations. However, as time went by, I witnessed so many churches compromising their God-given mission to the differing values set forth by the non-profit organizations. Churches have to focus on teaching the word of God continually and challenge its members to live according to God's word. The focus of NGOs were on programs and contemporary events. Instead of influencing the NGOs, NGOs were influencing the Cambodian churches. As a result, the Cambodian churches were losing their foundational identity. It has been very disappointing and sad to see the Cambodian churches losing the message of the gospel and its power."

10. Ministry with Peter Kong, OMF Missionary

After we arrived in Phnom Penh, Dr. Choo came and told us there were two Korean OMF missionaries in Cambodia. One was missionary

Hak-yeon Cho, who was doing church planting and kindergarten ministry in Leak Leung, Prey Veng Province. The other one was missionary Peter Kong. Missionary Kong planted a church in the city and his ministry was thriving. Dr. Choo and his wife were

Missionary Kong's (second to the left) ministry

also attending Jesus Village Church that missionary Kong founded. Dr. Choo invited my wife and I to the Sunday morning service and there I met missionary Peter Kong for the first time. He was the first Korean missionary whom we met in Cambodia. Pastor Kong's hometown in South Korea was the same as mine: Goheung, Jeollanam-do. His wife, Sun-ah Kim, was also an alumni of the same Maesan junior high school I attended. Because of these prior connections, missionary Kong, the Choos and we were able to form an intimate friendship from the beginning and do ministry together.

When we opened a dentistry at the CSI hospital, missionary Kong, who was the president of the Cambodia Korean missionary Association at the time, came and gave a congratulatory speech. When I asked him to recommend a high school graduate who would be a good candidate to receive our scholarship to come to National Dental School, missionary Kong introduced Hun Buntha to us. Hun Buntha later became a doctor. Missionary Kong also managed a bachelor house, so he knew a lot of young people.

Missionary Kong also introduced us to a lovely young lady, Leakhena. Leakhena graduated from college while working as an assistant, and is currently working as a manager for missionary Byung Seol

Chung's mobile dental ministry. Just as importantly, when we opened our for-profit dental clinic, missionary Kong introduced us to a sincere sister named Seila. In her family, Seila was a daughter among many sons to her parents, who were very wealthy. She was staying at missionary Kong's bachelor house because her home was very far from school. She majored in accounting and later became the directing receptionist in charge of finances for our for-profit clinic. Because of her excellent work ethic, she was such a reliable person. She met a faithful college student from Prey Veng at the bachelor house. Missionary Hak-yeon Cho wanted to send him to seminary in Philippines. When her mother adamantly opposed this marriage, Seila obstinately stated that she will live by herself for the rest of her life. Finally, her mother gave in to Seila and she approved their marriage. Now, she is in the countryside doing church and kindergarten ministry with her husband. Although I was very sad personally to let go of such an able employee at our clinic, I was very joyful because where she was going was also God's mission field. As a tangent, before marrying her loving husband, Seila got hired at a bank by her father's arrangement. However, she resigned after only 2 weeks. Everyone was very surprised that she did this since it was normally very difficult to get hired as a full-time employee. Seila shared that she felt no joy during the 2 weeks working at the bank, so she returned to the ministry field where brothers and sisters in Christ were working together. Seila's decision to pursue the real treasure of the gospel, in spite of a world that pursues money and material things, was such an inspiring lesson for me.

Missionary Kong also went on the portable dental missions with us 3 times whenever short-term dental teams from Atlanta, Georgia, came to Cambodia. Dr. Hwang donated a digital X-ray and computers with compatible software, and we put them to great use during portable dental missions. Missionary Kong planted 3 churches in Cambodia. Every church planting was successful. As he later became the director of OMF

Korea, he handed over all the churches to local pastors. Whenever I think about my beloved missionary Kong, I remember his generous heart and his helping hand towards many missionaries with his thorough understanding of Cambodian culture. I also remember him as a great church planter. It was such a blessing for me to spend time with him and work together in Cambodia. He was a huge encouragement and inspiration to me in my walk of faith.

11. Dr. Yewon and Chern Chern Choo

During a vision trip to Cambodia in January 2004, CDS arranged an interview with OMF dental missionaries Dr. Yewon and Dr. Chern Chern Choo.

Dr. Choo became the most crucial partner for my dental ministry in Cambodia. They were the ones who taught me the reality of dentistry in Cambodia. They also connected me to a Christian dental school graduate, who later ended

Dr. Yewon and Dr. Chern Chern Choo

up working with me. The graduate's name is Dr. Sokha Meas. He was a senior at dental school and was the only Christian among the students. They also connected me to a student who I was able to teach and to share the gospel with. Both Yewon and Chern Chern were working at the only National Dental School (total 25 students) in Cambodia.

Drs. Yewon and Chern Chern Choo came from Malaysia in 1996. They came very early during the period when the door to missions in Cambodia first opened. They were very young and spoke fluent Khmer language.

His wife, Chern Chern, was especially talented in language. Her out-

Dr. Choo lecturing on implants

going personality helped her interact with the locals very well. At one time, she was in charge of evaluating the newly commissioned OMF missionaries' progress in language acquisition. Dr. Chern Chern felt burdened by the fact that Cambodia didn't have any orthodontics specialists, or even available orthodontics classes. So, she went to Singapore and after studying for 3 years, came back as an orthodontic specialist.

The Choos also connected me to Christian Dental Association of Cambodia. There, I was given an opportunity to teach once a month. The Christian Dental Association of Cambodia's meeting was held at the largest church in Cambodia called New Life Church. Dr. Choo also sent all the families and missionaries of OMF to my ADC for-profit clinic to help support our business. Drs. Yewon and Chern Chern Choo attended the church that was pastored by OMF missionary Peter Kong. They also let me use the new digital X-ray machine, which was donated from an American church, at ADC clinic. They would always borrow the machine for portable dental missions and then return it every time.

Dr. Yewon taught at the Bible study that was held at our ADC for-profit clinic. He led the Bible study so well with his language fluency. His Bible study slides were always very well made. Dr. Chern Chern Choo also made delicious cheesecake like a patisserie and brought us joy. From the very beginning when we did our interview until our retirement, we were great partners in Christ. I never could have dreamed God would prepare such wonderful partners. Thank you, Heavenly Father!

12. Missionary Peace Chelvanyagam

Peace is a single missionary from OMF who was a specialist in oral surgery. She is an Indian-Malaysian and has also worked as a dental professor in Malaysia. I'm so grateful for Dr. Peace because she taught oral surgery skills to Dr. Makara. She checked and diagnosed oral surgery and oral cancer patients at my CSI dental clinic and for-profit dental clinic.

Peace, OMF missionary

Missionary Peace is serving as the professor of IU Dental School Oral Surgery Graduate program. She is a gentle soul, who is very intelligent and well-learned.

13. Myung Ja (Sonya) Maddock and Her Good Friend Jung Im Lee.

Sonya is my younger sister. She has a very outgoing and lively personality. Her personality reminds me of my grandmother. Sonya came to Cambodia 7 times: 3 times with Diamond Canyon Christian Church mission teams, and 4 times with Inland Korean Presbyterian Church mission teams. She attended both churches, going to the 8 a.m. service at Diamond Canyon Christian Church with her husband Gary, and then the 11 a.m. service at Inland Korean Presbyterian Church.

Sonya and Mrs. Jung Im Lee provided haircut services for women and children of the Cambodia mission team. Along with the haircuts, they would also apply treatments for hair lice, and washing. They were also prayer partners of our dental clinic that served the poor. After the missions team left to return home,

Sonya Maddock (right) and Jung Im Lee (left)

Sonya (first row, second from the left) and Jung Im (first row, last)

they stayed behind to pray for the sick at Mercy Medical Center. In 2014, they prayed for a man with terminal stage lung cancer. And after they shared the gospel with him, he accepted Jesus Christ as his Lord. A few days later, he died while they were still doing prayer ministry. The man left behind a wife and 4 children. The oldest child was a high school senior girl. Mrs. Lee introduced the daughter to her brother Kevin Kim, who was able to help her obtain a 2-year scholarship.

Sonya and Jung Im also served in SOPA (meaning "trumpet" in Hebrew) Korean Drum Ministry. This ministry integrated the gospel message into performances of singing, dancing, chanting, and drum beats. Sonya continues to serve as a team leader. Every year, SOPA team visits Burundi, Africa to partner with missionary Pastor Paul Shin and Mrs. Joy Shin who are doing ministry to those with leprosy. They are sponsored by Diamond Canyon Christian Church. Sonya is an official missionary of this church.

14. Ulsan Daeheung Church and Pastor Heungbin Lee

I received most of my ministry's financial support from the United States. The only support from South Korea was from Ulsan Daeheung Church (Presbyterian Church of Korea, Tonghap). They supported our ministry greatly. How I got connected to them was very unexpected. My mother-in-law, who has since passed away, was living at a senior apartment community in Koreatown, Los Angeles, and attending Lighthouse Mission Church. She attended the seniors prayer meeting and regularly interceded for my ministry in Cambodia. Pastor Heungbin Lee of

Daeheung Church in Ulsan and Pastor Sung-il Choi of Lighthouse Mission Church Missions Department were seminary colleagues. One day, Pastor Heungbin Lee asked Pastor Choi to introduce him to a missionary to support. Pastor Choi, then, recommended me to him. Daeheung Church was already supporting 10 part-time missionaries, but I was the first one from Cambodia.

The emeritus Pastor Heung Bin Lee at Daeheung Church in Ulsan

After I was connected to Pastor Heungbin Lee, I submitted my resume and waited for their response. Finally, an interview was held and Pastor Lee approved support for my ministry. He also held an elders board meeting after Sunday service and introduced my dental missions ministry to the elders board. The elders board unanimously approved. After about a month, two missionaries and I were officially commissioned through a send-off service. From that moment on, Daeheung Church in Ulsan faithfully supported us and became a great help to our ministry. On December 15, 2019, reverend HeungBin Lee retired and became the Pastor Emeritus at Daehung Church. Now, reverend KiHyun Kim serves as the sixth senior pastor.

My successor, missionary Dr. David Koo, was commissioned to Cambodia following the same process as I went through. However, after a year of ministry in Cambodia, Dr. Koo went to the Kurdistan region in Iraq through YWAM International. Daeheung Church in Ulsan is still supporting Dr. Koo in Iraq to this day. In whatever way, it is such a joyful thing to God for the gospel to be spread far and wide. Whether it is in Cambodia or Iraq, we will obey as the Holy Spirit leads. Amen. Come, Lord Jesus!

Minorities of Cambodia

Cambodia, with a population of 15 million, has 24 tribes living in the mountains of the eastern region. Among them, Bunong tribe has a very special relationship with our missionaries. Their population of 37,500 is comparably large among the other minorities. They live in Mondulkiri Province which is located at the border between Cambodia and Vietnam. There are Bunong tribes people living in Vietnam as well. Since the tribe speaks the same language, Cambodian and Vietnamese Bunong interact very regularly.

The Bunong tribe accepted the gospel message very well because they were very superstitious. Among the Bunong villages, Oreyang, also known as Jesus Village, was a place that David Everitt of our missions department went often to minister.

The name Jesus Village was given after all of the 50-60 households, except for 2, in this village believed in Jesus.

During the first portable dental mission to Oreyang, our team had to go through a very rough road. Then, we went to Busra village 2 times and Dadam church once. A total of 4 times, we were able to serve the Bunong tribes from various villages.

We had portable dental treatments for the wealthy farmers 4 times. They wrote hymns in the Bunong language using the Vietnamese alphabet. Their traditional housing was a hut made out of thick palm leaves. In order to keep the house from the cold, the doors and windows were very small which caused many to have eye diseases. Today, almost everyone is living in a regular house. Busra, the largest village of Bunong tribe, has a church (Vihear Nom Paug Chi Vet) of 500 members. The senior pastor of Vihear Nom Paug Chi Vet is Chintin. Another church, Vihear Lumper, has 300 members and the senior pastor's name is Yantrol. Amazingly, the whole village are members of these two churches. Whatever the Lord wills, He will make it happen!

Ratanakiri Jarai tribe lives in the northern part of Mondulkiri Province. Our team also went to their village 3 times and helped with missionary Kreg Mallow's (OMF) church-planting efforts. Wycliffe (Bible translation ministry) is currently translating the Bible into the Jalai language. Their current housing is made out of upgraded wood. I pray earnestly that the ethnic minorities of Cambodia will come to Christ and enjoy His love and blessings.

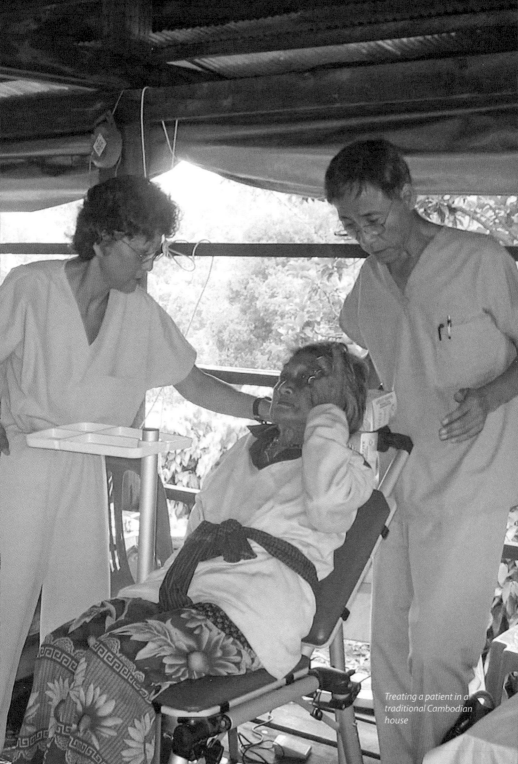

Treating a patient in a traditional Cambodian house

"

But you, keep your head in all situations, endure hardship, do the work of an evangelist, discharge all the duties of your ministry. For I am already being poured out like a drink offering, and the time for my departure is near. I have fought the good fight, I have finished the race, I have kept the faith. Now there is in store for me the crown of righteousness, which the Lord, the righteous Judge, will award to me on that day—and not only to me, but also to all who have longed for his appearing. (2 Timothy 4:5-8, NIV).

14

Dreaming of a New Vision

14 Years in Cambodia!

All the years of ministry that passed were completely due to the grace of God. We would not have been able to get through any difficult moments, or even do ministry, if not for the grace of God. During those 14 years of ministry, we just kept our hands to the task and kept moving along in our ministry journey. Now that we have come to the finish line and can reflect upon our ministry, I confess that my plans and the plans that God wanted were vastly different.

Before I went to Cambodia, my vision and my plan was to teach at the National Dental University in Cambodia. Yet, what God had pre-ordained for us was not teaching but providing healing and treatment to the poor and underprivileged. The last 14 years in Cambodia, interacting with and treating people

Big roots crawling into Angkor Wat temple

who neither had teeth nor toothbrushes, were years of blessing upon blessing, grace upon grace. I was able to handle all things with a joyful heart, and thankfully in 2009, God opened the door for me to finally teach at the International University (IU) School of Dentistry. I really enjoyed doing ministry with the young people of Cambodia. I cannot deny that ministry was hard—ministering and working in the dental clinic, in the university, and even the portable dental clinics. Nonetheless, what a joy and reward it was to go around with the portable medical/dental clinic, meeting Cambodian students and locals, sharing the greatest news of Jesus, and planting the gospel truths into their hearts!

When we were facing financial difficulty in the mission field, God opened an opportunity for us to do Business as Missions (BAM) by operating a for-profit dental clinic. This enabled us to be financially secure, which enabled us to also travel and operate the portable dental clinic abundantly. It was an unexpected, yet wonderful, gift from God for our ministry. It was solely through God's help and grace that I was able to hand over my dental clinic to Dr. Makara when I wrapped up my ministry in Cambodia. Dr. Makara, who was my local ministry partner, became a Christian when I shared the gospel of Jesus with him! I am deeply moved and thrilled to hear that the dental clinic operated by Dr. Makara is doing well even to this day.

It is my hope and prayer that, using the money they have earned, they may go to remote places that do not have dental clinics and treat the locals there with the portable dental clinic. Without faith, this is a ministry that is impossible to do. I pray earnestly that the Lord may give Dr. Makara a deep and abiding faith in God so that he may be able to handle this ministry well. I also pray for Leng Chan Heng, a great evangelist, that his rice shop will do abundantly well with God's help. I lift up in prayer 4 women, who, because of their faith in Jesus Christ in a Buddhist country, were not able to get married. I pray that God may send godly Christian bridegrooms so that they may have a Christ-exalting, God-glorifying family life, yet still. Although I shared the gospel with countless dental students over the years, the fruit of this labor was very small. However, I labor fervently in prayer for the day that the seeds of the gospel that were sown, will spring to life and sprout and bear much fruit!

On December 17, 2017, my wife and I ended our ministry in Cambodia and returned to our home in the United States. On that last day in Cambodia, during our farewell party, Dr. Makara shared his testimony. I was so overwhelmed by his testimony—it moved everyone to silence—and moved me so much in appreciation. When I recall and dwell upon my beloved Dr. Makara's testimony, it still moves me to tears.

Dr. Makara and his family

Makara's Testimony at the Last Farewell Party

My name is Dr. Makara. I first met Dr. Cho when I was a graduating dental student at the National Dental School. Dr. Sokha Meas, my best friend and classmate, introduced me to Dr. Cho 5 months before my graduation and I began to work with him since then.

I come from a very devout Buddhist family. Therefore, on the very first day of work, it was very strange and weird for me to see the people at the dental clinic singing hymns and having Bible study. It was my first exposure and experience seeing such a sight! The dental staff would sing songs, read the Bible, and talk about God with one another before the starting an hour of work. These activities would repeat every single morning. My purpose for working at this dental clinic was to pick up and learn dental skills from Dr. Cho and earn money for my tuition. I received $75 each month, working there part time until I graduated from dental school. After graduating, I began working as a full-time dentist at the dental clinic. While working there, I even went out to far countryside villages with Dr. Cho and his portable dental clinic. As I saw Dr. Cho and his team members working ever so passionately to treat the poor and the underprivileged, I began to be moved in my heart. It was difficult for me at first to understand Dr. Cho—he had devoted a considerable amount of both time and money to the portable dental clinic ministry.

I sometimes wondered why Dr. Cho would ever give up and leave a luxurious and comfortable life in the United States to come to such a poor country, laboring and facing all kinds of difficulties to treat underprivileged people. I simply could not understand it. It did not make any sense to me! Although I did not fully comprehend Dr. Cho, I enjoyed working with him. Why was that the case? I think because I also enjoy helping other people. It is my personality. I would often ask myself why I had to take on such a difficult task while working here. My cohorts were working as dentists at more famous and prestigious dental clinics. They were making considerably more money than I was. My friends would suggest and propose that we should work together. My heart would waver every single time. I realized later why I could not readily and willingly accept such amazing offers and why I needed to go on an alternate route. It was because of Dr. Cho's hidden passion and pure, unconditional love for Cambodia. I came to this conclusion: If Dr. Cho can help my fellow Cambodians without receiving any kind of compensation, how could I, as a Cambodian myself, not help my own countrymen? It was a given that I had to walk this path.

While working with Dr. Cho, I saw his clear and determined leadership. I would wonder and ask myself, "When he leaves and I am without any supervision, whether I would be able to lead brilliantly like Dr. Cho?" There were times when Dr. Cho would rebuke, admonish, and reprimand us with stamping on the floor. But I came to see and realize that all of this was done out of genuine love for us and to motivate us to do better next time.

Year 2007! At long last, after Dr. Cho's direction and evangelism, God touched my heart and I accepted Jesus Christ as my Lord and Savior as well as receiving baptism. Everyone, including my friends and family members, were extremely upset and unsettled by the fact that I was working at a dental clinic for a poor missions agency. All of them thought I was making a huge mistake not working somewhere else where I could make more money and become wealthy. But now, I, as a child of God who has been called by Him, do not have a shadow of a doubt of what God's good and perfect will is for me. If God had not led Dr. Cho into my life, I might have been more successful and rich in life, but I definitely would not have heard the gospel of Jesus and be a Christian today.

Finally, I would like to share with you a Bible verse that I know and remember. I remember the words of Jesus Christ in Matthew 16:26 (NIV), "What good will it be for someone to gain the whole world, yet forfeit their soul? Or what can anyone give in exchange for their soul?"

May God bless Dr. Cho and his family with an abundance of blessing! We will never ever forget Dr. Cho and his family and remember them eternally. Thank you so much.

Sincerely, Makara.

In 2019, acting upon the advice of Kennth K. Kim (member of Korean American Christian Dental Missions, now Global Dental Alliance), I wrote this small book. Kennth K. Kim, who was my mentor, had said, "Help our successors by leaving a record of your journey while your memory is still vivid." That is the reason why I wrote my dental memoir from Cambodia. With the help of Pastor Andy Sunwoong Kim, the president of Mustard Seed Bible Institution, from March of 2019, I began to write my memoir. During this time, from May to August, I went on a teaching mission trip to Ethiopia. From September 1, 2019, I travelled through the land of the Exodus, Egypt, for a period of 15 days. It was not until April of 2020 that I was able to complete this small book.

Oh My Beloved Cambodia!

Through the process of writing this book, I had a chance to reflect on the past 14 years of ministry. How could I ever forget all the missionary co-workers and dental staff who labored with me, rejoiced with me, and cried with me? How could I ever forget countless Cambodian people

that I met through the
portable medical/dental
clinic? How could I ever
forget all the people of
God who have support-
ed me and my dental
missions through prayer
and financial support? I
cannot help but confess
that all of this has been
the result of the grace of God!

Farewell dinner with school professors

We give all the glory to God who has protected and provided for our dental missionary journey every single step of the way. It is my hope that all the stories told in this small book, even if in the slightest way, would benefit all those who come after me who are planning to retire and pursue dental missions in the future.

Even in the year 2020, with the difficulty that the COVID-19 pandemic has brought about, "Missio Dei" (God's mission) will continue. I am so excited to see where and how God will use me and lead me. I strongly confess and proclaim the subject and the focus of all missions work is God Almighty. The wiseman states in Proverbs 16:9, "In his heart a man plans his course, but the LORD determines his steps." (NIV). This verse has now become the anchor and foundation of my life.

The heart of God the Father for the country of Cambodia has now become my heart, and must be the heart of the church in these end times. I am still running towards the scattered and lost tribes and people groups of this world—the ones that God yearns for to be brought back to His fold. I am praying without ceasing. Till the day that my Lord Jesus comes back, I will run with the gospel in one hand and my dental skills in the other, towards the goal of world restoration. I am

Dental mission team that came to Cambodia from Orange Hill Presbyterian Church (home church)

utterly convinced that the only hope for this world is the gospel of the cross of Jesus, and His resurrection. Therefore, it is my prayer and hope that this small book may be used in any way for the people of faith who are captivated by the vision and dream of a new birth, and new revival of worldwide missions.

"But you will receive power when the Holy Spirit comes on you; and you will be my witnesses in Jerusalem, and in all Judea and Samaria, and to the ends of the earth" (Acts 1:8, NIV).

He who testifies to these things says, "Yes, I am coming soon." Amen. Come, Lord Jesus. The grace of the Lord Jesus be with God's people. Amen (Revelation 22:20-21, NIV).